RECESSION CHALLENGE

Ramesh Kumar Tehlani

Edited by
Dipavali Debroy
Economist

UNICORN

Publishers
UNICORN BOOKS
J-3/16 , Daryaganj, New Delhi-110002
☎ 23276539, 23272783, 23272784 • *Fax:* 011-23260518
E-mail: unicornbooks@vsnl.com
Website: www.unicornbooks.in
www.kidscorner.in

Distributors
Pustak Mahal, Delhi
E-mail: info@pustakmahal.com
Website: www.pustakmahal.com

Branches
Bangalore, Mumbai, Patna, Hyderabad

ISBN 978-81-7806-164-1

Edition : 2009

Printed at : Param Offsetters, Okhla, New Delhi-110020

Acknowledgement

"Our best thoughts come from others.", as Ralph Waldo Emerson had said.

Writing a book or article or any piece like this requires help from a lot of people. I especially want to thank economic experts from the globe, who helped me to understand the concept of Recession and shared with me their ideas for survival in the financial crisis.

It is my first attempt of collection and compilation of such piece of knowledge work. I want to thank my friend Sanjay Lahoty, Shahin Akhtar, Vinod Gautam, Mayank Bhatnagar, Ajay Bhardwaj, Ms. Surbhi, Mrs. Neena Sharma, my Wife Sarita and others who motivated and supported me directly or indirectly to do so, I want to give special thanks to Mr. Ashok Gupta, Director, Pustak Mahal, who shown trust and interest in my topic and gave me opportunity and guidance to explore the world of writing.. And I want to express special gratitude to Mrs. D. Debroy (Editor of the book) for her more than needed support, without her support the book was incomplete.

Ramesh Kumar Tehlani,
24-B/40, Behind Police Chowki,
Adarsh Nagar, Ajmer-08.
Email – ramesh.tehlani@gmail.com

Contents

INTRODUCTION

- Lehman brothers files for Bankruptcy

BusinessLine , 15 September, 2008

- AID SLOWDOWN?

The Times of India. 2 March, 2009

- Rs. nears 52 against dollar, a lifetime low

Times Business, 3 March, 2009

- Coming soon: Zero inflation with everything but food going cheap?

The Times of India, 13 March, 2009

These days the most discussed about news is the present financial crisis that has surrounded the global economy. Almost every day the main headline of all newspapers and news channels is about our declining share markets, falling industrial growth and the overall depressing mood of the economy. For many people an economic depression has already arrived whereas for some it is just round the corner. In some experts' opinion the depression has already arrived and it has started showing its impact on India.

The fear of a recession becomes obvious over the United States and world and as it was said in last century, whenever the US sneezes, the world catches a cold. This is obvious from the way the Indian stock markets crashed taking an indication from a probable recession in the US and an overall global economic slowdown. Weakening of the US economy is not good news, not just for India, but for the rest of the world too.

The financial turmoil has preoccupied virtually everyone over the past few months. It is clear that we are in the midst of an economic slowdown. It might turn to recession. Some even think it might lead to a depression. Either way, it's going to be a tough ride, so objective of this piece of knowledge is to provide some information about recession and strategies for surviving the crisis posed by recession.

So make no error about it, a recession is here. India's growth rate in October –December 2008 was only 5.3%. Inflation rate was less than 1% in March, 2009, and may even turn negative These are the characteristics of recession.

While we do not know how long it will exist or painful it will be, we do know that it has the potential to be the worst financial crisis any of us have ever lived through. The stock market has lost more than 50% in the last 12 months. Investors witnessed erosion of their hard earned money and capital. Retirees and those nearing retirement have seen their nest egg eroded, some by 50% or more. And the banking and financial system is under severe pressure in the United States and globally. That's the bad information.

So that was a little about recession. Now why challenge? Challenge is a positive word and it motivates us to do something more and extraordinary to fight with the situation or circumstances. Something more, something new and something different.

And current recession is a challenge for all of us. Human race is capable of doing anything which is proven in history and it is not the first time we are facing recession. History had witnessed more than 10 recessions or depressions in last 100 years. And we survived. It is because we took it as challenge, we kept a positive attitude and did something extraordinary.

So again we are in front of a global financial challenge. And we have to fight and survive in such a financial crisis. And I trust we can do this.

THE WHAT AND WHY OF RECESSION

These are some definitions given by experts –

- A recession is a decline in a country's gross domestic product (GDP) growth for two or more consecutive quarters of a year. A recession is also preceded by several quarters of slowing down.

- Recession is a period of general economic decline, part of the usual business cycle.

- Recession is a significant decline in general economic activity extending over a period of time.

- Recession is a stage in a Business Cycle or Trade Cycle that signals a downturn in the activity level of the economy. The downturn is not yet serious enough for it to be known as a Depression. Output, investment, aggregate demand and employment all tend to fall in a period of Recession.

So recession is reflected in a decline in the Gross Domestic Product, or rather, in a decline in the economic activity that poduces the G.D.P.

What is Gross Domestic Product (GDP)?

Gross Domestic Product is the value of all final goods and services produced in a nation in course of a year. It is the broadest measure of economic activities and the principal indicator of economic performance. It is the total value of a country's output, income, or expenditure produced within a country's physical borders. When we look beyond the physical borders, that is, take into account income generated in foreign countries by people or property of the country concerned, as well as income of foreign countries being generated within the country concerned, we have the concept of Gross National Product. When Depreciation or wear-and-tear expenses are taken out of the GNP or GDP, we have Net National product (NNP) and Net Domestic Product (NDP). Out of these related concepts, GDP is the one most used as a measure of the level of economic activity going on in a country.

To be regarded as a recession, a decline in GDP must be over a period of at least six months. It is usually noticeable by job layoffs, soaring joblessness, reductions in retail sales, and the slowing of housing and car markets. Recession is the stage of economic declines, an extensive downturn in Gross Domestic Product, employment and business. As the decline in sea level before a tsunami, Recession is a natural caution sign that a tsunami is approaching.

Hence, economic recession is a phase of the business life cycle when economic activities start on a decline lasting for more than a couple of months. Such a decline is spread across the economy and is normally visible in GDP, employment, real income, industrial production and wholesale or retail sales. A recession in one country may be caused by, or may itself cause, recession in another country with which it trades.

But what is a Business Cycle?

Economic activities usually pass through four stages or phases of the Business Cycle – Recession, Depression, Recovery and Boom.

When GDP and the employment are declining, the economy is said to be in a recession, which, when deep becomes a depression.

When output and employment are rising, the economy is said to be in a phase of recovery, which becomes a boom as full employment level of output is approached and industries operate at maximum capacity. Booms are often inflationary periods.

An economy which grows over a period of time tends to slow down the growth as a part of the ordinary economic or business cycle. An economy, on average, expands for 6-10 years and tends to go into a recession for about six months to two years. A recession normally takes place when consumers lose confidence in the development of the economy and reduce spending.

An Inflation, let us be clear, is a period of rising prices (as distinct from high prices). It occurs when not just a few specific prices are rising, but the general price level is doing so. It is measured by an index that combines all the prices of all the relevant commodities and services in the country. There are several methods of calculating this index and the index itself has several variations.

In the diagram in the following page, time is measured on the horizontal axis, and the GDP on the vertical axis. The highest stage of the boom is called the 'Peak' and the lowest stage is called 'Trough'.

A Recession starts when the 'Peak' is passed and the downward movement towards the 'Trough' begins. When the upward movement from the Trough starts, Recovery is beginning. Recovery leads to Prosperity or Boom. But once the Peak of Prosperity is passed,

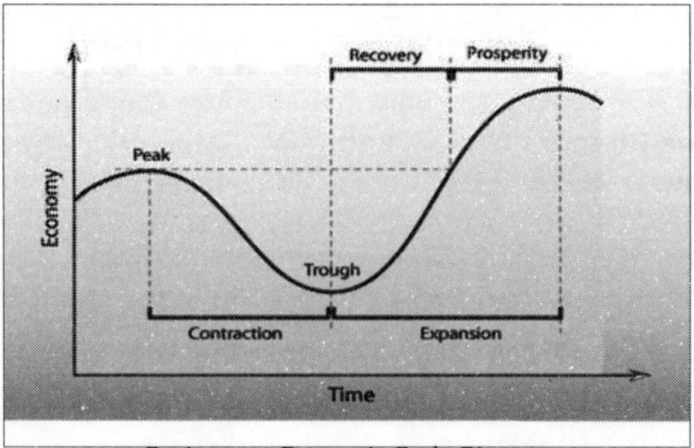

Business or Economic Cycle Diagram

the downturn may start again, the economy approaches Recession again.

A recession generally lasts for one to two years during which the rate of unemployment while rising is generally below 10 percent. These unemployment figures can vary in developed and developing countries. In developing countries like India unemployment rates generally (in boom period also) remain higher than developed countries like US and European countries. In recession periods it increased by approx 10 percent. It can be 10 percent for US and it can be 20 percent for developing countries.

When a recession remains for more than three years and /or the rate of unemployment lies (or rise by such rate in developing countries) between lies above 10 percent and 20 percent, the economy may be said to be suffering from a depression.

When unemployment remains high and business declines for six or more years, the nation is said to be experiencing the 'Great Depression'.

Indications of recession vary in different countries. For example, if GDP growth in India falls by 2 to 3 percent, it can be recession for India. But for developed countries like the U.S.A., if GDP growth falls from 1.5 percent to 0.5 percent or zero, it can be recession for the country.

A recession has many characteristics that can be found to manifest themselves at the same time and can include decline in immediate measures of overall economic activities. A recession is the result of fall in the demand and may be connected with declining as well as rising prices (and stagnant output).

An extended or severe recession is referred to as an economic depression. Although the difference between a recession and a depression is not clear, but it is often believed that a decline in Gross Domestic Product or GDP of more than 10% constitutes a depression. For example, if GDP of India come down to 0% or less than 0%, then Indian economy will be called in depression.

AFTER WHAT AND WHY, WHEN AND HOW?

Some Recession Theories and Recession History

There were no recessions or depressions before the Industrial Revolution in England and the emergence of Capitalism. Recession, Depression, Recovery, Boom, that is, the Business Cycle is a feature or characteristic of the Capitalist society.

Classical economic theory was based on the assumption of Full Employment. The economy was assumed to have enough demand for all the products it produced. This idea was neatly expressed in what is known as the Say's Law: Supply creates its own Demand. JB Say (1769-1832), a Classical thinker, put it in this neat form.

With the rise of factory industry and mass production of goods using mechanised technology, it soon became clear that supply did not always create its own demand. Textile industry in England started off the Industrial Revolution in England in the late 18th century. But by mid-19th century the Lancashire cotton mills were beginning to lose their steam. It was the rise of the railways which then gave the Industrial Revolution a new lease of life, and saved it from slipping into recession.

But in the next century, in the late 1920's rolling on to the 1930's, the recession could not be staved off. After the First World War, the advanced countries of the West began to slow down and there occurred what is known as the Great Depression.

The Great Depression started in the USA (like the current recession) and then spread to UK and other European countries. It affected colonies of the British Empire, that is, it affected India as well.

Geoffrey Trease gives an account of it in his book *This Is Your Century* (1965, William Heinemann Ltd)

"There were no shortages in 1929 .Farmers were producing more food than they could sell, shops were full of goods which people wanted but could not buy, factories were silent because it was useless to make more goods until some had been sold. The farm-hand shivered without the coat he could not afford, which the unemployed garment-worker would gladly have made, so that he could buy farm produce for his hungry family. In bygone centuries, when life was simpler, such men would have bartered among themselves. In the complicated modern world they were helpless.

"This was the general predicament everywhere, not shortage but surplus, production beyond the point at which crops and goods could be sold at a profit, men had worked so efficiently that they had worked themselves out of their jobs.

"........Conditions got worse. By 1932 there were more than 32 million unemployed, 5000 banks had closed their doors, and the nation's income had been halved. Depression gripped the country. It was a time of breadlines and soup kitchens, silent factories and shuttered sores, men trying to sell surplus apples on every other street corner." (pp161-164)

It was then that J M Keynes (1883- 1946) put forward his theory in the book *The General Theory of Employment, Interest and Money* (first published in 1936).

Brilliantly he showed how Aggregate Demand (AD) in the economy could fall short of Aggregate Supply (AS), leading to unsold goods piling up. Wages being `sticky' or slow to change, the producers (the capitalists) could fight this only by reducing the production, that is, by throwing people out of jobs and causing unemployment on a large scale.

When AS (Aggregate Supply) is more AD (Aggregate Demand), there is Recession / Depression. Most of the pioneering thoughts in this area are from Keynes. It is this area or branch of Economics that is known as Macro-economics.

Macro and Micro Economics

Macro-economics studies the economy's aggregate or total output, employment and the price-level, in contrast to Micro-economics which studies production, consumption, distribution from the point of view of the individual unit (be it household or firm)as though under a microscope.

Around the same time, in fact a little earlier, another economist, Joseph Schumpeter had come out with a theory of Business Cycles ("The explanation of the business cycle", Economica, 1927). It contrasts with the Keynesian theory because it puts its emphasis on industrial innovations rather than banking or other monetary factors. Another contrast is that it starts by explaining the boom or prosperity rather than the trough of recession/depression. .

Citing examples from history, he argues that `innovations' or technological progress it is that cause capitalist economies to boom, and when such innovations become old and accepted and a matter of routine, the burst of economic activity they had caused, begins to flag and die down, causing a downturn of the business cycle and developing into a recession or depression. When new innovations are made, the economy picks up again and the upswing of the business cycle starts. Thus the cause of recession/depression is non-monetary; it is related to technological advance – or, the lack of it.

Booms, he says, consist in the carrying out of innovations in the industrial and commercial organisms. By innovations he means major or substantial changes in the combinations of the factors of production. They consist primarily in changes of methods of production and transportation, or in changes of industrial organisation, or in the production of a new article, or in the opening up of new markets or of new sources of material. The recurring periods of prosperity of the cyclical movements are the forms progress takes in a capitalist society.

He goes on to argue from economic history from, say, 1760 onwards that very many booms are unmistakably characterised by revolutionary changes in some branch of industry which, in consequence, leads the boom. Railways, for instance, in the 1840s, or steel in the 1880s, or electricity in the '90s...."

Schumpeter's position is stated very clearly: Booms and consequently depressions are not the work of banks, their cause is a non-monetary one and entrepreneurs demand is the initial cause even of so much of the cycle as can be said to be added by the act of banks.

Macro-economic theory has moved much ahead of Keynes and Schumpeter. But it remains firmly rooted in Keynes and Schumpeter.

Reality : the Recession that is here and now

Now I shall talk in plain terms about the current recession

- First, it is very much there in India.
- Second, it is there in the rest of the world too.
- Third, it had its start in the U.S.A.

Now let us begin from the third point rather than the first.

What had started it off in the U.S.A.? What was it there that has led to this major economic disorder in the world that has stock markets declining all over world and major banks becoming insolvent ?

In an interview to NDTV (on 18 October 2008.) right before the Presidential elections in the USA, Nobel prize-winner Amartya Sen had said: it is loss of confidence that has pushed the US into a recession.

"It (US) certainly is in a recession already. There is no question about that. The question is how deep a recession it is," he told NDTV.

When asked about his assessment of the US economy, he said that the current recession there was "shallow". Sen emphasised that it was not caused by "some gigantic external problem" but due to the loss of confidence by the American people in the system.

"And that is usually how recessions happen. You lose confidence, you cut down your activities and as a result others cut down their activities," he said.

Past Recessions in the U.S.

It is not as though this is the first recession in the world or even in the US. The US economy has suffered several recessions in the past. We have already talked of the Great Depression from 1930 to 1939. It was a decade of high joblessness, low earnings, low prices of goods, low inflation and high poverty. It affected the world markets in the 1930s. Agriculture and Mining suffered the most. In 1937, the activity level of the American economy fell all of a sudden, the fall lasting through most of 1938. Manufacturing declined sharply, as did profits and employment. Unemployment jumped from 14.3 per cent in 1937 to 19.0 per cent in 1938.

But this was not the end of the story.

The US experienced a recession in 1982-83 due to a tight fiscal policy to control inflation and sharp correction to overproduction of the previous decade. This was followed by Black Monday in October 1987, when the stock market fell and the Dow Jones Industrial Average fell by 22.6 per cent affecting the lives of millions of Americans. The early **1990s** saw a collapse of junk bonds and a financial crisis.

The US saw one of its biggest recessions in **2001**, ending ten years of growth, the longest on record. From March to November 2001, employment dropped by almost 1.7 million. In the 1990-91 recession, the GDP fell 1.5 per cent from its peak in the second quarter of 1990. The 2001 recession saw a 0.6 per cent decline from the peak in the fourth quarter of 2000. The dot-com burst hit the US economy and many emerging economies as well. The economy also suffered after the 9/11 attacks. In 2001, investors' wealth fall off as stock prices in IT crashed.

So the US has gone through several `fits of depression' before the one that has it now in its grip.

Current Recession

There are various fundamental causes behind the current economic recession. Primary among them are the positive regulatory norms in US that resulted in steady economic growth and development without showing any signs of decline, eventually ignoring the fundamental nature of business cycle of the economy. Low inflation rate over the last two decades gave a speed decline during the downturn phase of the economy.

In the beginning of year 2007, the first signs of recession were visible when USA was struggling with surplus liquidity which today bubbled out as price inflation and real estate bubble. Even investment banks were flying higher with higher risks compromising highly leveraged business. The type of risk undertaken proved to be disastrous for them, as they were not able to gather the required amount of capital to support their flying risks and leveraged transactions. Even the size of the investment banks played a vital role in down fall of the economy.

The recession began in the U.S. and then got interlinked with other countries, including India. Let us take a look at what was happening in the housing sector of America for past several years.

In America, a boom in the housing sector was driving the financial system to a new level. A combination of low interest rates and big inflows of overseas money helped to create easy credit environment where it became fairly easy for public to take home loans. As more and more people took home loans, the demands for property increased and fuelled the home prices further. As there was sufficient money to lend to prospective borrowers, the loan companies started to expand their loan disbursement reach and make the loan conditions more and more hassle-free.

The loan executives and agents were asked to find more potential home buyers in lieu of enormous bonus and incentives. Since it was a good time and property prices were high, the only intention of most home finance companies and mortgage firms was to give loans to as many potential customers as possible. Since almost everyone was driving by the greed factor throughout that housing boom period, the common sense practice of examining the customer's repaying capability was also overlooked in numerous cases. As a consequence, many people with small income and bad credit history or those who come under the NINJA (No Income, No Job, No Assets) class were given housing loans in disregard to all philosophy of financial caution. These types of loans were known as sub-prime loans as those were are not part of prime loan market (as the repaying capability of the borrowers was unsure).

Since the demands for homes were at a record high, many homeowners used the increased property value to refinance their homes with lower interest rates and take out another mortgages against the additional value of home to use the funds for consumer expenditure. The lending companies also lured the borrowers with attractive loan schemes where for an initial period the interest rates were low (known as Adjustable Rate Mortgage (ARM). However, regardless of knowing that the interest rates would increase after an initial period, many sub-prime borrowers opted for them in the expectation that as a result of high housing prices they would be able to quickly refinance at more favourable terms.

Bursting of the Bubble

On the other hand, as the saying goes, "No boom lasts eternally", the housing bubble was to burst sooner or later. Overbuilding of houses throughout the boom time finally led to an excess stock of homes, resulting home prices to decline starting from the mid of 2006. Once housing prices started depreciating in several parts of America, refinancing became more difficult. Home owners, who were expecting to get a refinance on the basis of increased home prices, found themselves unable re-finance and began defaulting on loans as their loans reset to higher interest rates and payment amounts.

In the US, an estimated 8.8 million homeowners - almost 11% of total homeowners - had zero or negative equity as of March 2008, meaning their homes were worth less than their mortgage. This provided a reason to "walk away" from the home than to pay the mortgage.

Foreclosures (i.e. the legal procedures initiated by a creditor to repossess the property for loan that is in default) accelerated in the United States in late 2006. During 2007, nearly 1.3 million U.S. housing properties were subject to foreclosure activity. Growing foreclosure rates and unwillingness of many homeowners to put up for sale their homes at reduced market prices drastically increased the supply of housing inventory available. Sales volume (units) of new houses declined by 26% in 2007 as compared to previous year. Further, a record nearly about 4 million unsold existing homes were for sale including nearly 3 million that were vacant. This excess supply of home inventory placed considerable sliding pressure on prices. As prices declined, more homeowners were at possibility of failure to pay and foreclosure.

Now you must be wondering how this housing boom and its consequent turn down is interrelated to current economic and financial depression? After all it appears to be a local crisis of the US.

What Complicated the Matter?

Unfortunately, this problem was not as straightforward as it appears. Had it remained an issue between the lenders (who disbursed risky loans) and unpredictable borrowers (who took loans and then got defaulted) then possibly it would remain a local problem of US but, this was not the case. Let us see what complicated the problem.

For original lenders these subprime loans were very profitable part of their investment portfolio as they were estimated to yield a very high return in view of the growing home prices. In view of the fact that, the interest rate charged on subprime loans was about 2 to 3% higher than the interest on prime loans. It was due to their risky nature of sub-prime borrowers. Lenders were over confident that they would get an attractive return on their investment. In case a sub-prime borrower continued to pay his loans, installments, the lender would get higher interest on the loans. And in case a sub-prime borrower might not pay his loan and defaulted, the lender would have the alternative to sell his home on a high market price and recovered his loan amount. In both the conditions the sub-prime loans were excellent investment options as long as the housing market was flourishing. Just at this scenario, things started getting complicated.

With share markets booming and the financial system flushed with excess cash money and liquidity, a lot of large fund investors like hedge funds and mutual funds felt subprime loan portfolios as attractive investment opportunities. Consequently they bought such portfolios from the original lenders. In this way the lenders had new funds to lend. The subprime loan market thus became a fast growing sector. Major U.S. and European investment banks and institutions heavily bought these loans to diversify their investment portfolios. These are known as MBS (Mortgage Backed Securities). Most of these loans were brought as parts of CDOs (Collateralized Debt Obligations).

CDOs are just like mutual funds with two significant differences. First unlike mutual funds, in CDOs all investors do not share the risk equally and every participatory group has different risk profiles. Secondly, in comparison to mutual funds which normally buy shares and bonds, CDOs usually buy securities that are backed by loans (just like the MBS of subprime loans.)

Due to heavy buying of Mortgage Backed Securities (MBS) of subprime loans by key US and European Banks, the problem which was to remain within the limitations of US propagated into the world's financial markets. In an ideal world, the MBS were a very good options as long as home prices were increasing in US. It is like Mutual Funds which are good investment options as long as share prices increases. However, when the home prices started declining, the attractive investments in Subprime loans turned risky and loss-making.

As the home prices started declining in America, sub-prime borrowers found themselves in a messy condition. Their house prices were losing value and the loan interest on these houses was increasing. As they could not manage a second mortgage on their home, it became very hard for them to pay the higher interest rate. Consequently lots of them opted to default on their home loans and vacated the house.

However, as the home prices were declining speedily, the lenders, who were hopeful to sell them and recover the loan amount, found themselves in a situation where loan amount exceeded the total current cost of the house. In due course, there were no options but to write off losses on these loans.

The problem got worsened as the Mortgage Backed Securities (MBS), which by that time had become parts of CDOs of large investments banks of America and Europe, lost their value. Declining prices of CDOs injured banks' investment portfolios and these losses damaged banks' capital. The complication of these instruments and their broad spread to major international banks formed a situation where no one was too confident either about how big these losses were or which banks had been hit the hardest.

Turmoil in the Banks

The effects of these losses were massive. International banks and brokerages have had to write off an estimated $512 billion in subprime losses so far, with the largest hits taken by Citigroup ($55.1 billion) and Merrill Lynch ($52.2 billion). A little over half of these losses, or $260 billion, have been suffered by US-based firms, $227 billion by European Banks and a relatively modest $24 billion by Asian ones.

Despite efforts by the US Federal Reserve to offer some financial support to the struggling financial sector, it has led to the fall down of Bear Sterns, one of the world's biggest investment banks and Brokerage Company. Bear Sterns was taken over by JP Morgan Chase with some assistance from the US Federal Bank, the central Bank of America. Bear Stearns was the fifth biggest U.S. investment bank and had its headquarters in Manhattan in one of the world's tallest buildings which by itself was worth more than $ 1 billion. But its shares fell fast in value from a 52-week high of $159.36 (valuing it at $19 billion) to $ 30 in March 14, 2008 (valuing it at $ 4 billion). On March 16, J P Morgan Chase bought it off at $2 per share. What a fall!

The crisis has also witnessed Lehman Brothers – the fourth largest investment bank in the America and the one which had survived every major mayhem for the past 158 years - file for bankruptcy on September 15, 2008. Formed in 1850, this enduring symbol of investment banking collapsed in 2008. Its shares fell from a high point of $66 in February 2008 to less than $10 in mid-September.

Merrill Lynch has been bought out by Bank of America. Freddie Mac and Fannie Mae, two large mortgage companies of America, have effectively been nationalized to prevent them from failing. As per some reports insurance major AIG (American Insurance Group) was also under severe difficulty.

A chain reaction of panic started from this point of time. Since banks and other financial institutes are like backbones for other major industries and provide them with investment capital and loans, a loss in the net capital of banks meant a serious damage in their capability to give out loans for a range of businesses and industries. This presented a serious liquidity crunch situation for companies who wanted cash for performing their business activities. At this time it became very difficult for them to raise money from banks.What is worse is the reality that the losses suffered by banks in the subprime disorder have in a straight line affected their money market the world over.

Money Market and Recession

What is the Money Market?

Money not only helps in buying and selling but also is bought and sold in what can be thought of as a `market' of its own..

Goods and services are bought and sold in the Commodity Market. It is the price of a good that brings the demand and supply of it into balance or equilibrium.

Labour is supplied and demanded in the Labour Market. It is the wage rate that brings about balance or equilibrium between the demand and supply of labour.

Money is supplied and demanded in the Money market. It is the interest rate that integrates or equilibrates the demand and supply of money.

The Money Market is an inter-bank market where banks lend and borrow money between themselves to meet up short-term need for funds. Banks generally never keep the exact amount of liquid cash that they need to disburse as loan or credit. The 'inter-bank' market performs this important job of bringing cash-surplus and cash-deficiency. Banks get together and lubricate the process of credit release to companies (for working capital and capacity creation) and consumers (for buying cars, consumer goods, etc).

As the housing loan problem intensified, banks grew ever more doubtful about each other's solvency and capability to honour commitments. The inter-bank market shrank as a result and this began to harm the flow of funds to the 'real' economy and financial system. Panic spread in the system and as the loan market went into problems, it created problematic situations for other markets.

The liquidity crisis in the banks has resulted in a stretched situation where it has become tremendously difficult even for top companies to take loans for their requirements. A sense of doubt and intense precaution is widespread in the banking sectors. The global investment community has become extremely risk-averse. They are taking out of assets that are even slightly considered risky and buying things traditionally considered safe and secure – gold, government bonds and bank deposits (in banks that are still considered solvent).

By itself this financial crisis is the conclusion of the above mentioned troubles in the global financial system. Inter-bank markets across the globe have frozen over. The heavy turn down in stock markets across the world is a victim of this disorder.

Governments and central banks (as Federal Bank in US) are trying every trick in the book to stabilise the markets. They have pumped hundreds of billions of dollars into their money markets to try and unfreeze their inter-bank and credit markets. Large banking institutions have been nationalised. The American government has set aside $700 billion to buy the 'toxic' assets like CDOs that fuelled off the crisis. Central banks have got together to co-ordinate cuts in interest rates. None of this has stabilised the global markets so far. However, it is hoped that appropriate monitoring and controlling of the money market will sooner or later control the situation.

How Much?

THE IMPACT OF RECESSION

Global Impact

In the era of globalization, no nation can remain isolated from the fluctuations of world economy. It would be immature to imagine that crisis and recession in the United States would have no impact in other countries of the globe. Today, the world is facing an acute economic crisis. In spite of huge government initiatives in the US and other major developed countries, the economic crisis is spreading at a fast pace from the financial sector to the broader economy and affecting basic production in all sectors. The United States accounts for one-fourth of the world's GDP and any significant slowdown is bound to have after-effects elsewhere. The impact is being felt in almost all the nations.

Huge losses suffered by major international banks have naturally had an effect on all the countries of the world as these banks have their investment interests in almost all countries.

Today the whole world is facing the backwash of the American financial crisis. In many countries including India, central banks are working to improve liquidity but are charging higher credit. The interest rates had drastically increased from 11.5% to nearly 16% in the year 2008. People are afraid to put money into the stock market due to fluctuating markets.

The real estate sector is another victim of the current financial crisis. To cope with the falling market, real estate professionals are attracting prospective buyers with better and attractive offers and schemes.

The highest affected sector in US is banking and finance. Lehman Brothers eventually went into bankruptcy. Later on the US government announced Fannie Mac and Fraddie Mae to take over the Lehman Brothers in September 2008. AIG is another victim of recession and recorded a heavy loss. Another giant Merrill Lynch filed for bankruptcy and cut a deal for about 50 billion dollars with the Bank of America.

The situation has engulfed most of Western Europe. In the U.K., banks like the HSBC, the Standard Chartered, the Royal Bank of Scotland and Barclays are trying to recapitalise and the Bank of England is infusing liquidity through loans. Britain has seized control of Bradford and Bingley, a mortgage company. In Belgium, the government took partial control of the Fortis Bank, a bank whose liabilities are much larger than the GDP of Belgium. In Iceland, government has nationalised the three biggest banks of the country and in Denmark, on 24 August 2008, the National Bank took over the huge Roskilde Bank (founded in 1884 and having branches over most of the Capital Region and headquarters in Roskilde) after it had run into financial trouble.

In Japan, real estate companies are facing a severe setback and forcing regional banks to raise reverse against bad loans. Even the Detusche Bank has come within the tentacles of economic crisis. The liability of the Deutsche Bank is nearly about 80% of the GDP of Germany.

A depressing atmosphere, shortage of liquidity, fall in demands, falling growth rate and uncertainties in the market are some of the most noticeable aspects of an economic depression. What started as a small issue of sub-prime loan defaulters has now become a matter of global concern. This greediness of some has caused pain to billions.

Impact on India

The present US crisis is affecting Indian economy in a comprehensive way.

Stocks and Shares

In the last three years, our share market was moving to new heights, thanks to heavy investments by Foreign Institutional Investors (FIIs). However, when the parent companies of these FIIs (based mostly in US and Europe) found themselves in a severe credit crisis as a result of sub-prime problem, the only option left with these investors was to take out their money from Indian Stock Markets to meet liabilities at home.

FIIs were the main buyers of Indian Stocks and their exit from the market was certain to cause disaster in the market. FIIs who were buying last year are now selling their stocks in India. As a result our share market is close to the bottom level.

The Indian stock markets have crashed. Stock markets reflect the enthusiasm of the economy and lower profits mean lower dividends and so, lower enthusiasm. Because of the foreign companies pulling out their invested amount to meet high inflations and losses, stock markets in India have swung violently backwards.

The Rupee against the Dollar

While the money which FIIs get after selling their stocks in India needs to be converted into dollars prior to they can be sent home, the demand for dollars has all of a sudden increased. As more and more FIIs are buying dollars, the rupee is losing its power against dollar. As long as demands for dollars remain high, the rupee will keep losing its power against dollar.

Borrowings

The current financial crisis has also started directly affecting Indian industries. In the past few years, the two most preferred methods of raising capital by the companies were through share markets and external borrowings at moderate interest rates. Share markets are bleeding everyday and it is not possible to raise money there. Regarding external borrowing from global markets, this option has also become difficult.

Foreign Borrowing

In the last year alone, India borrowed $29 billion from foreign lenders and got $34 billion of Foreign Direct Investment (FDI). A global crisis has hurt external demand. Foreign lenders who have become very risk-averse can restrict access to international capital. If that happens, both the financial system and the real economy will get hurt in the course. All of a sudden, the 9% growth objective does not appear that 'doable' any more; we should be happy, if we achieve 7% growth in this financial year and the next.

Banking

Our banks are facing cash liquidity crunch resulting in a deficiency of liquidity in the market. The Indian Banking sector is facing a tough time. Lehman Brothers and Merill Lynch had invested a huge amount in the stocks of Indian banks that had invested in derivatives. Lehman Brothers and Merill Lynch being severely affected, there has been a severe impact on ICICI Bank, which had invested in Lehman's bonds. Even Axis Bank has been affected but at a smaller level.

On the other hand, one positive point in favour of India is the fact that Indian banks are more or less protected from the bad effects of the sub-prime mess. If we take a quick look at the balance sheets of Indian banks, it would be demonstrated that their exposure to complex instruments like CDOs is almost nil. In India, the major banking system and operations are still in the hands of the Public Sector banks who are excessively cautious in disbursing loans to needy people/companies. Consequently, we are not likely to see a repeat of sub-prime disaster in India. Although there have been the presence of large US/European banks in India and even some Indian banks (like ICICI Bank) have some foreign subsidiaries with stake in the sub-prime losses, their presence is very low as compared to the overall size of the Indian banking sector. So at least on this major front we need not be much concerned.

The Recession has made Loans more difficult to Get

In a recession, banks and financial institutions are less willing to lend. This is particularly a problem at the moment, because of the concurrent credit crises which is reducing the availability of loans. The primary reasons behind it are lack of liquidity and non-availability of money at moderate rate. Due to current crisis, almost all banks and NBFCs (Non Banking Finance Companies) of India have stopped personal loans and business loans disbursals.

The Recession has reduced Business Profits and affected Industry

Profits of industries directly linked to the global market have been affected and are likely to be affected further.

Information Technology and Business Process Outsourcing

In Indian IT companies, more than 50 % of the revenue come from banking and financial institutes. Because of this economic slowdown, banks and other institutes failed to yield sufficient revenue to such IT companies,. This eventually forced them to a crisis situation. The IT giants TCS, Wipro, HCL and Infosys Technologies are also in line for the same crisis.

Indian tech and Business Process Outsourcing (BPO) services industry is also hit by this crisis because it is strongly dependant on US. This has even increased the value of dollar against Indian Rupee, making the situation worse.

Telecom and Engineering

Telecom and engineering sectors are also experiencing the impact of the recession. Many organisations have melted down in the country. Many people have lost their source of income. New deals are not materialising. Recruitments have been frozen.

The Automobile Industry

The auto industry is hurt. Luxury car sales are down 13% and the auto industry can't even give away the big SUVs, because of skyrocketing oil prices. The credit crunch has also knocked a growing number of consumers out of the market, as lending guidelines tighten.

Aviation and Tourism

Aviation and Tourism industry can be vitally hit. Indian companies with big ticket deals in the US would see their profit margins lessening. Tour and travels companies are reducing fare and tour packages due to lowering of demand, but positive impact is not visible.

Pharma, FMGC and Education

Pharma, FMGC and Education industry are little affected. These industries are also called recession proof industries.

ITes, Financial Services, and Infrastructure

ITes, Financial Services, and Infrastructure companies' employees could face lay off. These sectors are major affected sectors.

Export Firms

The uncertainties for exporters will grow as rupee strengthens further against the US dollar. Remember, India's exports to the US have grown significantly in the last few years.

Consumer Goods

A global recession is likely to result in a fall in demand of all types of consumer goods. In 2007-08, India sold approx 14% of its goods to foreign buyers. A fall in demand is likely to affect the growth rate this year. Our exports may get affected badly.

In short, the US recession has definitely impacted upon the industrial sector. The rising pressure on companies to manage the situation has brought hands of fear, panic and adversity into Indian industry.

The whole of Asia would be hit by a recession as it depends on the US economy. Asia is yet to entirely decouple itself (or be independent) from the rest of the world, say many economists. Indian and Chinese economies are much stable compare to other Asian countries.

Impact on Housing and Real Estate

The housing sector in India is badly affected compared to the other sectors.

Indian real estate was a booming sector till year 2007. Within a span of 3-4 years the property rates were touching new peaks because of India's growing desire for property. Her booming economy, off-shoring businesses, and her IT growth were the reason for growing demand. The demand for urban housing had increased manifold because of multinational companies and prosperous families. Despite all the growth in real estate, this sector was (and is) fairly unorganised. Most of the housing deals lacked transparency. And prominent companies in this segment had put huge money for the further developments.

As mentioned earlier, the first signs of approaching recession in the US came in the form of US sub-prime loans. Housing and mortgage business turned into a disaster for many investment banks. That crisis was the initial sign of global slowdown that spread also to India.

The sustainability of housing projects in India became a question. Recession brought down housing demand from IT and commercial spaces. The net worth of individual investors too came down.

Lehman Brothers had signed a joint venture with some of the Indian real estate companies like Peninsula Land Ltd and DLF Assets. These have also suffered heavy losses.

Many private equity firms had invested large money in the real estate sector of India. Most of the real estate companies listed in stock exchange have witnessed significant erosion in their market capitalisation. Now it will take long time for this industry to recover.

Impact on Indian Job Market: the Recession has led to Unemployment

Unemployment is a direct consequence of recession. A downturn in economic activity records a direct dip in employment. This is the major concern over a recession. If demand for output does fall, there is likely to be a fall in the demand for labour. This problem is often concentrated in those sectors most affected by the recession. For example, in the current climate, jobs related to finance and the housing market are more at risk than, say, the manufacturing and healthcare sector. Almost everyday we are reading newspaper reports of lay-offs and pink slips in various industries and companies. Millions of employees have lost their jobs. Even the rate of hiring new employees is going down drastically, eventually changing completely the picture and nature of the job market.

In 2008 more than 100,000 jobs were lost in organised job market. The unemployment rate is more than 8%, the highest since 2003. Over the last six decades from 1948 to 2008, the rate of unemployment has varied from 2.5% to 10.8%. IT companies, BPO, private firms and even big multinationals have closed recruitment and are also firing old employees. Today, when the company is closed or facing slowdown, employees are at a stage of nervous tension. Professionals are now scared of changing their jobs and are even insecure in their present-day jobs. The situation has become so worse that the job class people are on the edge, without knowing which side are they going to fall.

The Recession has led to Loss of Consumer Confidence

The Recession has impacted on consumer confidence and created in people a fear about the future, partly because of media reports that have sometimes exaggerated the extent of the downturn in the economy.

Impact on GDP

The Indian economy is likely to lose between 1 to 2 percentage points in GDP growth in the next financial year due to current turmoil.

Amartya Sen on the Impact on India

Let me remind you of what Amartya Sen had said in the interview to NDTV on 18 November 2008. He had said that that it may take a few months to rebuild the US economy. Mr. Sen said that if the cards are played well and backed by "clear-headed, intelligent thinking" people it would be possible to turn around "a fairly shallow recession".

Mr Sen also emphasised that India and China are less affected for now as their economies are not so much dependent on global economy, but added that the booming sectors have "a clear trade connection and those will definitely be affected".

"In the long run we may be very well affected and we already are to a large extent," he said.

Asking the Manmohan Singh government to be careful, he said that the governments of India, China and Brazil can take up "a lot of initiatives" that will not only protect them, but also help in speedy recovery of the global economy.

More recently at Kolkata on 23rd February 2009, Amartya Sen said that India's annual growth could go down to six percent or lower due to the economic recession. But he added that while it could do so, he was not a fortune-teller. However, Sen was confident that India's growth would never decline to the level of Japan, which registered a negative growth of 12 percent.

Sen believed that increasing internal demand was a way of tackling the economic sloth. "To some extent that is happening because the government earlier wanted to reduce the fiscal deficit. But now they have decided not to do that. That itself is a stimulus package in US terminology," he told reporters.

Mr Sen said while raising internal demand was a way of dealing with the problem, there were limits to it, as some sectors like Information Technology and pharmaceuticals were dependent on exports.

He said that the economies of India and China have sustained despite the global meltdown. "To some extent, the Indian and Chinese economies are insulated from the global economy. This is good for India, as its trade with China is growing very fast," Sen said.

He traced the cause of the US recession to the removal of control in the financial sector, Sen, however, said: "India and China have not been susceptible to the same type of fragility that has affected the US."

He said the markets in US would go down further as they were yet to reach the bottom.

At the NDTV interview, October 2008, Amartya Sen had also said that he was hopeful that, if elected as President, Obama, the first black presidential candidate in the US history to turn around the economy. "His coolness is an advantage in the time of a financial crisis. When that happens, I think you will see the confidence turn around quickly," he stressed.

Well, Obama did win and is now the President. Let us see how long it takes him to turn things around.

At the moment, almost half-a-year after Amartya Sen had made this comment, the recession is not only there but has deepened as well as spread all over the world.

Kaushik Basu on Recession

Kaushik Basu, Professor, Cornell University and a recent Padma award-winner, has said in November 2008 that the recession engulfing Europe and America - and now Japan - is unlikely to be as deep as the Great Depression of the 1930s and this is because of China.

China is sufficiently integrated with the industrialised west to be able to provide support, and yet not so integrated to go down with it. Although China is expected to slow down this year, the most pessimistic growth projection is 8%.

Even for India, the Chinese economy is a bulwark and partly explains why India is expected to grow by around 7% this year, despite the global crisis.

Thus, as the experts say, the long-term scenario for India is stable. A weak dollar could bring more overseas money to Indian markets. Oil may get cheaper brining down price rises. Recession could bring down oil prices to $30-35 per barrel. And it happened in the beginning months of 2009.

The whole of Asia would be hit by a recession as it is linked to the world economy. But the Indian and the Chinese economies are much more stable compared to other Asian countries.

Jayati Ghosh on Global Crisis

According to economists C.P. Chandrasekhar and Jayati Ghosh, that the argument that Asia, as "decoupled " could serve as a shock absorber, moderating the impact of the crisis, was wrong. At the World Economic Forum, 2009, held at Davos, delegates came despondent and left in despair. Both the discussions and the new evidence released at and during the Forum indicated that the global crisis was not just bad, but worse than expected. A damaging projection from the IMF (in its January 2009 Update to the World

Economic Outlook) declared: "Global growth in 2009 is expected to fall to half per cent, when measured in terms of purchasing power parity, and to turn negative when measured in terms of market exchange rates.

India thus is not insulated from the global financial crisis. Like the rest of the world, we too have to think out ways of surviving it.

How to Survive A Recession

During one lecture Mr Sarthak Behuria, Chairman, Indian Oil Corporation Limited, had said very well, "Today were not like they had been before. Constant change is here to stay, which means that the future just isn't what it used to be. And it's time we wake up to the fact and move. Those who don't move will be left behind in the dust of economic history – and the only way to move is up or out. It is pointless to stand in the bedrock of profit-centred stability, in spite of the floods of change that sweep over us. We must be the best and lead the rest, whatever the cost."

With many predicting a recession, the average consumer may be worrying how a recession might affect them and what they can do to insure against the negative effects of recession. These are some of the strategies for recessions and how to deal with them.

Strategies for Businessmen

In the context of the global slowdown, entrepreneurship throws up many a challenge to the coming generations.

A new class of entrepreneurs is required to push business to greater heights of superiority in this complex global market. The paradigms are fast changing. In the context of climate change and environmental degradation, sustainability of businesses has to be given principal priority over the conventional objectives like profitability.

Already there is a shift in business strategies of Business community of India. Large IT and BPO firms have started looking at other markets like Europe and even the domestic market, to spread their risks and reduce the impact of the rising rupee. This can be best seen with Infosys and TCS setting up an India centric team. Indian companies will have to adopt multi-pronged strategies, which includes diversification of the export markets, improving internal efficiencies to maintain cost competitiveness in a stretched export market circumstances and moving the product portfolio up in the value chain to impart resilience.

The IT sector too is keen to defend its position. In case of a full-scale US recession, the onsite staffing business will see a drop in sales and margins. At the same time, they can increase the offshore assignments. Recessions at this stage may not last for more than two to three years. Smart companies will continue to make investments so that they can be ahead of the competition when the US economy comes out of recession.

This means Indian business community will have to spend a lot more to build up market and distribution links in alternate markets like Asia, South Africa and Europe. Experts say the export dependent sectors of the economy need to re-focus on local demand and income from non-dollar economies.

Indian IT firms can positively find good deals in domestic market, but the deal sizes are likely to be small. India has a vast small and medium enterprise base and it is the right time to tap this segment. As for automotive components, consumer electronics and mobile devices, they have already established a market in India and have also started looking at tie-ups in China and other Asian and African countries.

The European, West Asian and the African countries may offer feasible short-term alternatives to our export-dependent sectors. BPOs, for example, will have to re-negotiate with their clients and fix appropriate pricing for their services.

Strategies for Small Business Owners

Your business will, without doubt, be affected throughout an economic recession. If you don't find ways to make it ride out the storm, probability are you will have to file for bankruptcy and close. Luckily there are things you can do to keep it floating.

Keep in mind that the heart of every business is good customer service. If you give special treatment to your customers, these people will leave feeling satisfied and always come back. This is something that your employees must understand because if they don't, these individuals will be the first one to go since you have to cut back on your operating expense.

Another way of doing that is to retrain your staff. You can hold seminars on customer service or simply give them a refresher course of the products and services that you are offering because this will make an impression in the customer's mind the moment they walk in through the door.

Employee motivation is necessity at that time because good morale always achieves a favourable outcome. Being the business owner, you should lead by example by working longer hours at work. If they see you are doing whatever it takes to stay afloat, they will do the same because again, their jobs are on the line and they could loose their job if things get worse.

The majority of businesses think that letting people go is always the first option. You don't have to make the same mistake when these reductions can be made elsewhere as long as quality is not compromised. If you have to buy things, see if you can get longer credit periods or better rates; so large expenses can become smaller ones, making it easy to manage.

It is always nice to have customers pay in cash but during an economic recession, that is hard for the consumer. So if you don't use a credit card machine yet, now will be a good time to get one. Studies have shown that more people will be able to buy from you using a credit card especially during a time of financial downturn.

The primary aim of any business is to make profit, so part of surviving an economic recession will be also to lower your profit margins. By informing your customers of this move, they will be able to buy more at a very reasonable price. You can move up prices again when things get improved since such a crisis is only temporary.

In its place of relying on people coming through your door, you can also look at other ways to promote your business. One of the most affordable ones nowadays is the Internet; so create your own website. If you can't do this on your own, hire someone to do it and then make sure that is it both attractive and interactive.

Other businesses are also feeling the impact of recession and they are also doing their best to stay afloat. Ask around what they are doing and share the same information as well so that you will have other ideas and options when the ones you have right now do not work.

When it gets difficult to Borrow

In a recession banks are less willing to lend. This is particularly a short-term problem because of the concurrent credit crunch which is reducing the availability of loans.

- Solution: One should avoid taking on any unnecessary debts. One should try to reduce (if they have any debt) and consolidate into a lower interest rates bearing account.

- On the positive side, in a recession interest rates are likely to be lower, meaning lower interest payments for mortgage holders. Few days back RBI had reduced REPO rate which will turn down rate of interest of loans, which is a good step taken by RBI (REPO Rate - Whenever the banks have any shortage of funds they can borrow it from RBI. Repo rate is the rate at which our banks borrow rupees from RBI. A reduction in the REPO rate will help banks to get money at a cheaper rate. When the REPO rate increases borrowing from RBI becomes more expensive.) And we are waiting for another rate cut and more relaxations in the progress.

When Business Profitability is Falling

If you are a small business owner the decline in margins as impact of a recession can be felt clearly. Decreasing profits could even threaten the survival of the business.

- Solution: Find ways to minimise costs without compromising the business. There are always many ways to reduce costs and increase efficiency. Some economists even go so far as to say that recessions are a good thing because they force the economy to become more efficient.

- If your business is particularly affected by the downturn, look to see whether you can diversify to reflect the dynamic economic environment. For example, if you specialise in sales of luxury goods with a high margin try to include some new products which appeal to people's desire for frugality. Or in tough times when selling manufacturing machines has become challenge, try to find service and support as alternates to fight the sale drop. It might be possible it can become main source of income in crisis time.

• A fall in profits is part of business cycle. Therefore try to plan a financial plan to borrow at a lower cost for the challenging years.

There is no question that if you focused your business model on, say, residential or commercial office development, then things might be quiet. But, if your model is diversified and you have tentacles into more buoyant sectors such as health care and education (as Learning Skills Council), then you are likely to be in better position.

Recession Proof Business

There are some businesses which are either unaffected or very low affected by the recession.

Academic / Child-centric Businesses

Education is believed to be comparatively recession-proof. Most parents will reduce their own expenditure for the sake of their children, ones that are related with their children's future well-being and education. Tutoring services, music classes, and college-related education are some of the ventures that are not affected by economic slowdown.

Caretaking Ventures

Children, aged relatives, pets and basic household needs are some of the areas that need to be focused on at all times, irrespective of the economic environment. While some people might just reduce their caretaking expenditures during a recession, most of them will get rid of other non-essential services before cutting down their caretaking budgets. Thus caretaking ventures such as daycare providers, eldercare services, dog walking/sitting, and lawn care services are some of the businesses which suffer the least because of the economic slowdown.

Health Care and Pharma Businesses: Healthcare and related services are most essential business services just like educational services. They top the list of fast-growing businesses and are hardly affected by recession. Examples are : medical assistance, home health aides, physical therapists, physician assistance and medical records and health information technologies, etc.

Business Support Services:

Throughout tough economic times, businesses are inclined to reduce the use of non-essential service providers such as event planners or caterers. But most businesses still require the help of basic business support services such as accounting, financial consultancy, data entry, book-keeping , in order to continue running their everyday operations. Businessmen running such services are least affected by the current slowdown.

Online and Internet Services:

To cope with the negative effects of recession, entrepreneurs can change their business to adapt to different markets or to promote their services/products in the market of another country. Here "Internet business" can help a lot.

The various points why the Internet businesses are not affected by slowdown are-

- It provides to different demands for web products or services in various diversified markets.
- Its costs are much lower than those of conventional business. It involves only hosting and domain name cost which is much lower than the rental cost of conventional businesses.
- It deals in various currencies of various countries and enables one to deal with various countries.
- It involves low maintenance cost and no workforce once it has been set up. Generally by considering the above points most Internet and online business have escaped the main costs of

recession. Recently we had seen an increasing trend of bloggers and they are making good money just with blogging.

Strategies for Employees

It is said that "A recession is when other people lose their jobs. A depression is when you lose your job."

In the last few months, we had seen lay off news flashing on TV channels and newspapers. TCS, Jet Airways, Sony, Yahoo and many more companies asked employees to leave. Apart from these, salary cuts, poor percentage or no salary hike were some other steps taken by companies.

Are we conscious of this threat? Yes. But do we really care and see what the future has in store for us? Perhaps No. The young professionals still keep going on with their expensive urban lifestyle and they do not seem to bother about the economic recession. It looks like we are not prepared/ preparing for the worst. How about receiving a lay-off notice on a fine day morning in your office? Or a cut of 20-30% in your present salary? Can we survive? It will be a NO for most of us.

How do we tackle this situation? We might have to start from the very basics. I think the following might help:

√Reduce Expenses - Shopping, visits to expensive restaurants, air travel, etc.

√Long term savings and investments - Mutual Funds, Unit Linked Insurance plans, etc.

√No more loans – And no more EMIs. How would you pay the EMI if you do not have a job or if your current salary is slashed to 30%?

√Minimum usage of credit cards - Or even better, avoid it as much as possible.

If you fear unemployment, start thinking what you might do as an alternative. Is it viable to consider working on a second income, such as online business or freelancing. Also if you have a car and a two wheeler, you can perhaps give your car for rental and use your two wheeler for your personal use. Do not rent your car to a regular Rent-A-Car service as it can cause damages to your car because those who take cars on rent for picnics, etc. care nothing about the car. So it is better to rent it to NRI families visiting their hometown.

√Don't panic. Firstly, the unemployment may not occur; there is nothing to be gained by worrying over what we have no controls other.

√If you find yourself unemployed, the best solution is to be flexible in looking for work. Consider new avenues and skills that you could learn. Also, recessions are short-lived; a period of temporary unemployment does not have to become permanent.

√Freelance – outsource your talents, even if it is on a small scale. What do you do in your free time? Shopping? Going out with friends? Fine if you go out with friends to get rid of your boredom, but can you spare the fun for the weekend? And find some free time on the weekdays and some on the weekends too? If you can, freelancing not only lets you pick up the job that you would like to do, but it pays well too. But beware, most of the companies do not like their employees doing freelancing.

Here are a few points that you should consider before starting freelance:

• A good portfolio for demonstration: All your clients would be asking for your profile/portfolio before they award their project to you. And you should present (only) your best work before them. They will also ask for verification to make sure the work is done by you.

• Effective and fast communication: One thing that the foreign clients want to make sure is that you understand their project requirements. So you will have to go through the minute details of the project and convince them that you understand their need. A response like "I am confident that I can complete this project" blah blah blah won't help. Detail to them on how you can complete the project, what milestones you have set for the project, the deliverables of the project etc. Also it will help if you respond to the client emails/messages as early as possible.

• Set milestones for both project delivery and for payments so neither you nor your client gets disappointed.

√Be Ready For Layoffs: While we should do everything we can to keep our jobs, layoffs are unavoidable. And they might happen to me; they might happen to you. No matter how secure you think your job is, be ready for the unthinkable. This means having your resume updated, knowing what friends and colleagues you would get in touch with for job opportunities, and knowing where you would apply for a job.

√Protect Your Job: In a recession, your job should be priority number one. This may mean working in a few extra hours, working a little harder, and improving your expertise and skill. Those that stay employed during a recession generally weather the storm just fine. While the unemployment rate is still relatively low in India, it is very likely to go up. And the last thing you want is to be looking for a job with an unemployment rate of 8%, 10% or even higher.

How to hold your job in tough times

Just imagine, you're chatting with colleagues in the office over a cup of tea, a colleague comes up to you and says 'Did you hear? They're firing. It's already happening in sales function and they're saying it's going to hit all the functions one by one.'

This doesn't come as a total shock to you. You have seen the signs. There have been budget cuts, travel cutbacks, projects have been cancelled or kept on hold, managers have handed in their resignations, off rolls and contractors have been terminated; there have been reductions in support personnel; downsizing is out of control.

Times are difficult, the economy is facing crisis, and companies are simply not seeing the kind of profits they were enjoying a few years ago. Just last month you found out that your friend's whole team was asked to leave.

You have a bitter taste in the back of your mouth. You can't afford to lose this employment. You want this job. You know it's going to be hard to get such another job today.

On the other hand, you're fine at what you do. You're smart, hardworking, you earn this job and you're going to keep it! Never forget, they hired you because they need your skills and experience. So, how do you make sure that your job is not on the edge? Start with the intangibles aspects.

Have a positive outlook

No one likes to work with a person who has negative attitude. You have to show your optimistic nature, team spirit and self- starter approach. You have to demonstrate the passion about your job that you had shown to your boss during your interview.

The main thing is to be positive, act positive, speak positive and feel positive. Criticising or complaining about your salary or your company or your seniors will be negative approach in bad times, which will be harmful for you. If you are going to show or say something, they had better be things about working hard. Don't forget there are long lines of people with their resume, who can replace you and they are just waiting to grab the opportunity. Most importantly, never, ever say negative things about your job profile, timings, job pressure, colleagues or any other side of your job to, or within audible range of your boss or superiors. When making suggestions or bringing up issues that need attention, be neutral at worst. Be supportive and practical whenever possible. Avoid giving voice to your frustrations and blaming your co-workers.

Never lose your self-respect

If you feel the sudden urge for to make a bond with your boss, make it as real a bond as possible. Taking up smoking so that you can go along with the higher-ups on their smoke breaks is not only unhealthy, it also means that you're working less, not the kind of thing they want you to be doing. If possible, start taking a smaller number of breaks. The next time a senior pass through your desk at lunch-break time, you're going to be so busy with your work that you won't even notice them noticing your dedication.

Real hard work will pay you in long term. Coming before office timing and leaving late will give you added advantage. Do not try to do that the other way around. You want to be at work, at your work station, before your boss walks in, and you want them to see you at your work station, showing no signs of leaving, as they're walking out. That being said does not make longer tasks that were supposed to be finished and handed in yesterday.

Be friendly and admiring

Firing is often more subjective than objective. Unfriendly employees have double the chance of getting fired that do the employees who are popular among their colleagues and superiors. If you're the kind of person who is egoistic, don't help out a colleague with a problem, show off about their achievements, and usually have an unpleasant outlook, the probability is that you're going to get into trouble even if you are as good a performer as the next guy.

If you take the help of a colleague, don't forget to express your thanks to him or her. Every little effort contributes to keeping work atmosphere friendly. The first person that comes to one's mind in an optimistic and positive light is someone you like, not someone who is just competent. Things are never as bad as they appear and every down is followed by an up. Follow the simple rules and you will be well-prepared for whatever the employment market throws your way.

Multitask

It is common for employees who have witnessed a round of layoffs to feel paralysed or trapped, but that's the ideal time for them to reinvent themselves. Rough times often present the opportunity for employees to lay other skills to work, to multi-task, handle various responsibilities, even if to a small extent. Employees who posses multi-tasking skills not only help an organisation keep up the work pace, but make sure that they are more valuable to the firm and that's why less at risk in the next wave of lay off. If you're good at multi-tasking, and you feel you can do part of a laid-off colleague's job, go to the boss' office and let them know that you can help.

A volunteer spirit presents team-player skills and team-players support changing scenario. Taking on additional responsibility helps you gain insight into other aspects of the company, improve your knowledge of how the company operates and what skills other tasks need.

Be smart

It is vital that you keep track of information on current events. You need to know about changes in the economy that are going to affect the industry you work in. Reading helps a lot and it will be good if you are being aware of what is going on in the economic and corporate world today. Use this knowledge when you participate in office discussions, and keep your ears open to the opinions of those senior and wiser colleagues who are more aware than you.

Do not let yourself become inactive. During recession, it's all the more important that you stay on your toes. Be supportive of changes at the workplace, such as cost-cutting actions. If you can, even help your superior to plan a strategy to control costs further. This would not be a good time to put in a request for expenditure on training, or for holiday leave. Remember the *mantra* – work, work and work. Come across as someone who is hundred per cent devoted to the job..

Be organised and aware

Be organised, sharp, and quick on the job. Improve your resume. Many people work and take additional courses as well. You could either pick up an additional qualification or take a training course in a hobby. Unofficial information that comes through the company gossip is really your best bet to the state of the company.

Often the first clue that a company isn't doing as well as it should be will come through the gossip and the sooner you know, the more organised you will be for the time when rumours turn out to be fact. Do not however use the gossip to speak negatively of your colleagues. It will almost surely backfire..

Just Supposing You Get The Sack

In a recent piece in Times News Network, Norbert Rego suggested how to Survive the Sack!

- Avoid negative thoughts by using techniques like Yoga and Vipasana.
- Be in the company of positive people. Do not waste time on those who are always whining and watering down your dreams.
- Tell yourself that change is inevitable and can be for the better.

Recession-proof Jobs

But there are some jobs which are offering a ray of hope for job seekers.

BPO and off shoring activities are still providing new job opportunities.

Telecom and Internet have a good growth scenario. Telecom companies are still adding millions of new telecom and broadband customers and signs of recession are not visible in this field. There are various jobs available in this sector including marketing, sales, processing and technical job, etc.

FMCG (Fast Moving Consumer Goods) sector will be providing new job opportunities continuously.

Environment related businesses will also provide the employment opportunities in coming future. Many companies are going green and there will be demand for new professionals with knowledge of cost effectiveness and green drive factors. Government, NGOs, laboratories and educational institutions, etc . will be in regular need of such professionals.

Actuary and Insurance sales are also recession proof jobs. Penetration of insurance in India is still not significant and professionals are still in short supply here. Insurance companies are hiring new sales force for their business expansion and actuaries will also be in demand in the future.

Education and Healthcare sectors too are hardly affected by the current global crisis and in these sectors, the demand of employees will remain stable.

Strategies for Investors

Best *mantra* for investors in recession is : try to diversify your investment portfolio. In a recession, commodities such as gold often do well. Even in a recession, there can be good investment opportunities. Also bear in mind that stock markets can often be forward looking. For example, stock markets have fallen sharply since the start of the year in anticipation of a recession. When a recession comes, stock markets often don't fall any more.

Don't Panic: I am simply amazed at the panic selling on in stock market that we have seen in the last one year. We read book after book that tells us that selling out of fear is the worst thing one can do, but we do it anyway. If there was ever a time for clear, rationale decision making, it's now.

Saving and Investing during a Recession

1. Don't stop saving for retirement: One thing about any investments during the market decline is that we should not sell

any of investments which have been done for long term and for retirement fund. One should not reduce the amount of contribution to pension plans or similar fund. As Warren Buffett would say, I'm trying to be "greedy when others are fearful." Although it is not easy keeping money in the market during a free fall, but selling out of fear is a sure way to lose buckets of money. Whether you invest in a provident fund or even pension plan, keep investing.

2. Reorganise your emergency fund: It is more important now for every one to have an emergency fund. How much is always the question. I think 6 months is logical and practical but it depends on many factors. If you are married, do you both work? If so, you might get by with 3 to 4 months. Do you have assets you can sell if you had to? We have two cars paid off and could sell one if necessary. Whatever your situation, building up your emergency fund is critical. I would keep it in a FD linked saving account or in liquid fund.

3. Don't rely on a credit against home or securities: This point is critical. You may have available credit on your home equity or on security like stocks, but did you know the bank can eliminate that credit? Go find your home equity line agreement, and you will see that if the value of your home falls or your financial situation changes, the bank can reduce the amount of your available credit.

4. Reduce unnecessary expenses.

5. A recession is an ideal time to take small calculated risk. This is an ideal time to acquire wealth as everything is at a cheap price. Keep on buying real estate and/or equity systematically. Don't buy at one go. Buy in small quantities.

6. Remember sectors that were looking good in the last boom will not be attractive in the next boom, so look for the upcoming sectors.

7. Make your portfolio diversified because at this time one does not know which company or sector will come out on top.Be aggressive in investment rather the defensive.

8. The real estate sector has witnessed downturn due to recession. But from the point of view of buyers of house property and investors in real estate, housing prices have come down with reduced interest rates and it is offering good opportunity to those who want to have their own house in big cities. Property prices have witnessed a correction of 20 to 30 % and some more is expected in near future. So if you are looking for a new house, it is an ideal time for you.

This is the time when capital is reorganizing itself for next boom. It is also the time when one should go in for self analysis. One should take into account what is good and what is bad. Recession is a natural process of penalising the industry that is worthless for the society. Only the best and the thing that is of use for the economy survives the crisis. Every investor should always invest in the company or sector that is at the core of economic activity rather than at the edge of the economic activity. Make this recession as an opportunity to build your fortune.

Recession proof Investment (in stocks/Sectors)

The economic turndown of 2008 has affected several industries. The biggest symbol of downturn can be seen in the way stock market had gone down drastically since the all time high in January 2008. A lot of investors have lost their hard earned money in the global meltdown. Stock prices of most top companies are at significant discounts. In fact, many of the sky touching stocks are priced at 1/10th value of their all-time high. Recession made many investors poor but if we see the positive side of this, then it is giving us new opportunities to invest in quality and fundamentally sound companies, which are available at very low prices.

It is sensible to invest in defensive stocks during the economic slowdown. It is a safer strategy for investors. Defensive stocks will not give sky-high returns but they will provide consistent returns with safety. Due to stability factor defensive companies are better in recession time.

There are some positive points of having defensive companies' stocks as they provide consistent growth, improve balance sheets and risk of loss is less. FMCG sector is most defensive sector. In last few years FMCG had shown consistent sales growth and same is expected in coming years. A practical investor always looks at FMCG sector due to its increased focus on farm sector which result in the growth in revenues from the rural population. Demand for consumer goods always remains steady. Chances of fall in demand are very low. Investors can look for those companies which deal in household care, hygiene product, hair care, chocolates and confectionary and so on. Stocks like ITC, HUL and Dabur are good investment options in FMCG sector.

Telecom, Capital goods, Engineering, Liquor and Oil and gas are other recession proof sectors. Almost all telecom companies are continuously increasing their subscriber base. Millions of new customers are taking new cell and connections. The slowdown is not visible in this sector. Airtel, Idea, Larsen and Toubro, BHEL and Reliance are good bet in recession.

Engineering goods segment is without doubt facing impact of recession in current scenario but given the fact that India will be needing large contributions in infrastructure, including power, road, ports, etc. definitely promising well for this industry.

Oil and gas plays an important role in any country's economy. India is heavily dependent on crude import. But with finding of new gas reserves and rise in refining capacity, this sector is also going to be an out performer in coming years. In the time of recession these sectors are prime for investment objective.

STRATEGIES FOR ALL

There are some common starategies to fight with recession challenge. These apply to all. By adopting these strategies we can survive this recession in a better way.

1. Pay down high-interest debts such as credit cards and personal loans. This should be an absolute priority. Credit cards can charge interest of up to 50 per cent and minimum payments will simply not pay the balance off quickly enough. If you lose your job or business scenerio is negative, the last thing you need are debts accruing interest at such a pace.

2. Overpay on the mortgage or Home loans. This is sensible at any time but giving yourself a financial buffer on your biggest financial commitment is more important than ever. If you lose your job or business is facing tough times due to slowdown, having a buffer which allows you to draw down on some extra capital, or miss a few mortgage payments, will be invaluable.

3. Don't change your mortgage to fixed rate. Interest rates have just come down by 1.0 to 2.0 per cent and the signs are they will come down even more. Now is the time to go variable, not fixed.

4. Ask a mortgage agent or financer about refinancing. In spite of the credit crunch, there are some excellent deals available, especially from small size lender and building societies. Among the top 10 best variable rate mortgages, the big banks don't appear at all. All the best deals are from the smaller lenders. Don't be scared to switch to them if it will save you money.
5. Go for Health insurance. This is one industry where competition is fierce, so use a good financial consultant or online comparison service to find you the best offer and services. If you have bought other types of health insurance such as Total Permanent Disability Insurance, you may well find it is cheaper through your company. They often offer members and employees discounted rates. Check with your employer.
6. Cut down on eating out or take-aways.
7. Go once a week to the grocery shop instead of making several smaller trips : buying in bulk will save money. Don't miss discounts given on bulk trade. Nowadays almost all retail outlets are giving huge discounts on bulk purchase.
8. Quit smoking and Alcohols. The financial crisis is as good an excuse as any to give up the cigarette and save money. If you don't smoke, take a breather from alcohol for a while and get thinner as well as richer. If you don't drink alchohol, you are right.
9. Reduce Spending: This is obvious, but it is important to recognise that there are many ways to cut spending. For example - Did you know that most mobile services come with different tariff plans? I switched mobile plans of my family members from post paid to pre-paid and saving almost 300 rupees a month and have not noticed the change. There are literally thousands of ways to save money (separate strategies are given on how to save money in tough time). Pick those that work for you, and start saving now. As part of this, seriously consider a cash back credit card. If you pay

off your balance every month, these cards are a great way to reduce your expenses by getting as much as 5% or more back on your purchases.

10. Don't invest in new capital. Don't invest in new business proposals without proper study and market survey. Although recession is good time for new start ups but if it is done systematically and carefully. Establishment costing is comparatively remains low.

11. Don't change jobs, as companies will retrench based on 'last in first out'.

Don't let Recession break up Relationships

The current economic recession can have quite another impact. Recession can be the reason for break up in relationships, even homes. During tough times, when one is worried about his/her career or job, it is very tough to keep romance alive or pamper one's life partner and/or children.

In Western countries like US and Europe, this has actually been happening. There is a general feeling of defeat in the air. Relationship counsellors and even psychiatrics are getting calls from disturbed people from all age groups. Arthur H. Goldsmith, the Jackson T. Stephens Professor of Economics at Washington and Lee University, has, as a part of Behavioral Economics, worked on the psychological impact of unemployment.

With the current economic crisis, Goldsmith points out that while there is fear on many different levels -unemployment, preparation for retirement, about being able to provide for children especially those nearing or enrolled in college. "The situation right now is fraught with the potential to have a great impact on the overall emotional well being of American society."

In India too there is the possibility of this impact. India is not insulated from either the economic impact or the psychological.

Am I going to be thrown out? Am I still going to be as attractive in his/her eyes when I no longer have my job? Should we stop thinking about getting married now? Should we postpone having babies? These are some of the questions young men and women may be having. Engagements and liaisons are reaching a breaking point.

Perhaps this is a good thing. If you chose your fiancé or even your spouse primarily for his worth in terms of income and assets, it is better that the relationship erodes with his worth. If you feel like dropping him/her because he/she can no longer afford dinners and parties, please do so. It is better for both of you. Happiness does not depend upon money, even upon jobs, and the sooner you realize this, the better,

But if you two can face the tough times together, if you can share your troubles and get the better of them, why then what does a recession matter? You will feel top of the world even at the bottom of the business cycle! In fact, the recession will bring you two closer together and provide the basis for an enduring relationship.

When money is tight and the stress level is high, that is when you know – whether you are really made for each other.

Relations apart, just by yourself, well, don't let Recession pull you down. Don't let Depression take you over. Call a friend. Share your worries. There are people willing to listen to you. There are people you can listen to. If you do not want to open up to relations, colleagues, friends and acquaintances, there are non-governmental-organisations that are there to listen to you. There are many websites on relationship counseling, which are offering free consulting.

TIPS FOR TOUGH TIMES

A few weeks ago I was not feeling good about the high expenses on everything. Recession or not, things are getting harder to afford. This is when I thought about how we can save money in tough times.

The tips are in categories so as to make it easier for you to find what you're looking for.

Save Money in Grocery or Retail Shopping

- Always purchase grocery with a list.
- Take advantage of sales on items that you would normally buy.
- Only shop once a month.
- Keep a price book and track prices by unit cost.
- Stock goods when prices are low.
- Buy generic (non-branded) items.
- Plan meals according to what is on sale that week.
- Take advantage of discounts at retail chains as Reliance Fresh, Spencer, More, etc. but only if you'll use the item.

- Buy enough of a sale item to last 3 months. That's about how long sales take to cycle.
- Shop at discount shops.
- Bring your own bags to the grocery store. Many stores offer a small discount per bag. And even it is good for environment if you bring cloth bag or Jhola.
- Take advantage of stores that offer coupons.
- Watch out for deals on things that your friends need, and have them do the same for you.

Save Money on Cooking and Eating

- Eat less non-veg. food. If possible become a vegetarian.
- Cook large amounts and freeze extra for busy nights.
- Scrape out food jars to use the last little bit.
- Eat from your stocked pantry.
- Bring lunch from home (it's worth it to invest in proper containers).
- Don't use the vending machines at work.
- Always have a meal plan.
- Keep soup starter jars in the freezer. A little leftover this, a little leftover that. Nothing is wasted.
- Get creative with leftovers. Think up new recipes.
- Don't drink soda. Drink water!
- If your kids complain about generic cornflakes, put the generic in a name-brand box. They'll never know the difference!

- Make your own baby food.
- Always take a snack and bottle of water wherever you go. You won't be tempted to stop for expensive fast food or drinks.
- Cook with the crock-pot to avoid using the oven, which warms up the house.

Save Money on Cars and Fuel

- Do household tasks once a week and use the most efficient route.
- Walk as much as you can.
- Stay home as often as possible.
- Keep tires filled to their proper pressure.
- Don't suddenly stop or accelerate.
- Ride your bike.
- Use a diesel or LPG/CNG car if you have one.
- Use public transport.
- Try to get by with one car if you have two.
- If you have one car that you only drive a couple of times a week, consider getting rid of it and using cabs.
- Drive your car until it's old. This works really well when you buy a car that will run for 200,000 kilometers.
- Keep up on your car's maintenance.
- Turn your car off at lights.
- Limit city driving.

- Turn off the engine at red light signal. (Only do this if you know your car and know what you're doing. It could be unsafe, depending on the car)
- Make it a challenge to see how far you can go on a full tank of Gas/Petrol.
- Fill up early in the morning when the air is cool, and the gas is dense. You'll get more gas and less air. It is true with Petrol too. In the morning you will get more because the temperature is less.
- Fill up when your tank is half empty.
- Shop around for insurance. The rates can vary a lot!

Save Money on Utilities

- Turn off every electrical item at the plug every night.
- Keep the lights off during the day.
- Don't use hot water in the summer.
- Consider a family plan for mobile phones.
- Use CFL bulbs.
- Don't run the heater at night.
- Open windows on summer nights to cool down the house.
- Use a fan.
- Get rid of your land line and use your cell phone.
- Take short showers.
- Shield your water pipes.
- Turn off the PC if you won't be using it for an hour or more.

- Use nightlights only when it's dark.
- Use nightlights in the bathroom, so if you have to use the bathroom at night, you don't have to turn on the light.
- Keep the freezer full. If you have to, put jugs or bowls filled with water in the freezer. It's less expensive to keep a full freezer cold than an empty one.
- Never leave the water running when washing dishes, brushing teeth, etc. Only use the water you need.

Save Money on Medical Needs

- Use a company's medical facility (if you are an employee) or try to take maximum tax relief by giving medical bills to the tax department of your company.
- Ask your doctor to prescribe generic medication.
- Buy generic medication. These medications are available at very low prices and are effective too.

Save Money on Clothing

- Limit clothes shopping. If possible shop at economy stores.
- Make the children change into play clothes after school to save washing and ironing costs.
- Re-use jewelry. If you lose a beautiful earring, put the one you have on a chain and wear it as a necklace.

Save Money around the House

- Use rechargeable batteries for electronics and toys.
- Store batteries in the refrigerator. They last longer.

- Do repairs (paint touch-ups, sewing, etc) one day a week. If you keep things in good working order, they last longer.
- Do home repairs yourself.
- Re-use things. An example: Plastic grocery bags can be re-used as lunch bags, shoe bags, or laundry bags on vacation.
- Ask stores for free samples. You can get some good stuff!
- Wash and re-use Zip lock bags.
- Make your own greeting cards by making a patchwork from the fronts of greeting cards you received the previous year.
- Use water from boiling eggs to water your plants.
- If you've bought stuff that you haven't used, see if you can return it.
- If you want to take a house or flat on rent, take it from a person, not a company. You're more likely to have some of your utilities paid, especially if your place is a room inside a house or a basement apartment.
- Move in with roommates or friends.

Save Money on Entertainment

- Stop magazine subscriptions.
- Use the library for books, magazines, and movies. See if you can reserve them online and then just pick them up.
- Read newspapers online.
- Celebrate "no spend" weekends, where you don't spend anything.
- Prepare special dinners at home, rather than going out to celebrate.

- Eat out only once a month.
- Do free things for entertainment: rock climbing, free city concerts, board games.
- Go to the park and have a picnic.
- Take advantage of "get in free" days at the museum, etc.
- To find special festivals, get a Free State tourism guide.
- If you find that you go somewhere a lot (zoo, amusement park), buy a season pass.
- Entertain at home. Have friends over for dinner, or have a game night and just serve snacks.
- Make your own "take out" style meals.
- Watching movies at home on DVD/VCD player instead of going to multiplexes.

Save Money on Miscellaneous Things

- Only get haircuts every 6-8 weeks, instead of every 4-5 weeks.
- Compost...it's good for the garden.
- Never spend change. Collect it and put it in a savings account.
- Don't watch TV. It cuts down on wants.
- Get rid of the TV all together.
- If you get a raise, don't raise your lifestyle. Save the extra or pay off your debts!
- Use a fee free credit card with rewards. Charge everything to get the rewards. But only do this if you are diligent about paying it off every single month. If you pay interest, it isn't worth it.

- Make sure you get the best interest rate on your savings, FD's, etc.
- Invest your money. Make it grow.
- Make monthly budget.
- Use a diary or worksheet to keep track of variable expenses.
- Use cash.
- Change your mindset. Instead of thinking "what do I need to buy?" think, "what do I have that I can use?" That's how people got through the Great Depression.
- Give stuff you don't use to others. It gets your mind off of your situation and onto others. And it promotes a sense of contentment and gratitude.

As you take steps to live a more economical lifestyle, think especially about last two comments. If you remember these two things, you will be well on your way to saving more money on day to day expenses.

Positive Aspects of Recession

If the last section has been too stark and gloomy, and you are feeling low, cheer up! There are some positive aspects too about recession ! If you look at the positive aspects, you will be better-equipped to fight with recession..

√Lower interest rates. During recessions central banks and governments of nations cut down the interests rates to stimulate demand and spendings. It is good for borrowers and small business owners.

√Lower inflation rates. In recession demand for goods falls. As result prices of goods also declines. It is good for savers.

√Lower stock prices. As discussed in earlier chapters, in recession we can buy stocks at very cheap valuations. Because of negative sentiments stock prices of even good stocks also declines. Recession is a good opportunity for-long term investors.

Sometimes difficult times can force us to reevaluate our financial situation. It can make us look for new business avenues and new ways to cut costs and spending. Although it may be temporarily unpleasant, the important thing is not to panic but try to make the best of any situation we find ourselves in.

SOME GOOD NEWS

There is no threat to the skilled people. According to NASSCOM India will have a shortage of about 5 million skilled people in IT and related sectors. So there will be lots of opportunities there still. Although there will be job cuts, it will be much less than in the US.

India's travel, tourism and power industry is going to grow at a higher rate. This is again a good sign.

This recession gives us the chance to be innovative. Our exporters can try various cost-cutting methods and tap new markets (such as West Africa where goods at departmental stores are sold five times the Indian price). It's an excellent opportunity for our exporters.

As Amartya Sen had emphasised that India and China are less affected by the recession as of now, as their economies are not so much dependent on global economy, but added that the booming sectors have "a clear trade connection and those will definitely be affected".

"In the long run we may be very well affected and we already are to a large extent," he said.

WHAT ROLE SHOULD GOVERNMENT PLAY?

Okay, but the strategies above are all for the individual – the individual householder, the individual investor, you or me, i.e. the private sector. What role has the Government got to play? What is the role of the Public Sector?

Before we go into this, we must explore an even deeper question. In recession or depression situations, DOES THE GOVERNMENT HAVE ANY ROLE TO PLAY AT ALL?

The very question seems strange to us. But let me tell you, the government's role in the economic life of a nation is not such a simple, straightforward matter.

In England in the 18th and 19th centuries, the dominant political and economic ideas were that of laissez faire. This French word literally means `leave alone' or `let it be'. It captures the essence of an economic theory or philosophy that the Government should not interfere in the daily economic activities of the citizens of a country, but only see to it that the framework of law and order is ensured. The State, according to this view point, is a policeman – not a participant. Except for certain essentials, all the goods and services in the economy should come from the Private Sector. In dealings with other countries, the policy of Free Trade should be followed.

Protection: tariff duties and such other measures should keep to a minimum. The market would decide what was to be produced, and sold at what prices and in what quantities.

This is, in effect, the philosophy of Individualism, and underlies much of the economic and political thinking of advanced capitalist countries, beginning with Britain. This is also the background of the Classical Theory which – as I have mentioned before – believed that Supply creates its own Demand and the government has nothing in particular to do to keep the two in balance. Just let things be, and the balance will be there.

This is why Adam Smith, the great Classical economist, had said that social welfare is maximised when each individual maximises his or her own individual welfare. Most of modern Micro-economic theory is based on this proposition. It may be added here , Amartya Sen, re-appraising of the works of Adam Smith in light of the current global economic recession, wrote in a recent New York Review of Books that free market with some amount of State regulation was what Adam Smith had advocated, not unregulated free markets, and in this, Adam Smith was right.

The Industrial Revolution in the 18th and 19th centuries and later the General Depression of the 1930s – changed a whole lot of things. A new kind of problem emerged – mass scale unemployment because there was a general lack of work, which, in turn, was because of lack of buyers who wanted the products of such work. Aggregate Demand (AD) fell short of Aggregate Supply (AS), to put it in the terms Keynes had introduced.

And I hasten to point out that Keynes did not stop at theory building. He said that in such a situation the State did have a role to play. When AD fell short of AS, why, the government had to do something about it. It had to step up AD by means of policies specifically meant to do so.

It is best here if I quote from a Professor of Economics at the Delhi School of Economics who is an authority on the role of the State in Economics. "Keynes Had A Point", Pulin B. Nayak writes (Times of India, 24 February, 2009):

"The Keynesian prescription ran counter to the orthodoxy of the day, and marked a revolutionary break from received modes of thought. But Keynes' persuasive power was formidable and among the earliest converts to his thinking – other than a close band of students and select professional colleagues - was President Franklin D Roosevelt. Roosevelt's *New Deal* ushered in a massive public works programme as per the Keynesian prescription."

What was the New Deal?

The New Deal was a set of plans and programmes that Roosevelt initiated between 1933 and 1938 with the goal of providing relief (work) to the unemployed, reform of business and financial practices.

The "First New Deal" of 1933 was aimed at short-term recovery programmes for all groups. The Roosevelt administration promoted or implemented banking reform laws, emergency relief programmes, work relief programmes, agricultural programmes, and industrial reform (the National Recovery Administration, NRA), and the end of the gold standard and Prohibition.

A "Second New Deal" (1935–1938) included labour union support, the Works Progress Administration (WPA) relief programme, the Social Security Act, and programmes to aid farmers, including tenant farmers and migrant workers. The Supreme Court ruled several programmes unconstitutional; however, most were soon replaced, with the exception of the NRA. The Fair Labour Standards Act of 1938 was the last major programme launched, which set maximum hours and minimum wages for most categories of workers.[5]

Most of the relief programmes were stopped during World War II by the Conservative Coalition (i.e., the opponents of the New Deal in Congress). Many regulations were ended during the wave of deregulation in the late 1970s and early 1980s. But some New Deal programmes still remain active.

The New Deal did succeed in helping the U.S. economy out of the Great Depression. It showed the world that Keynes was right that government activity was necessary to pull the economy out of doldrums.

As Pulin B.Nayak put it, "The Keynesian idea of having an interventionist state, particularly when economic activity was sluggish, remained the cornerstone of economic policy-making in the western capitalist world in the post-World War II era. For more than three decades the capitalist countries in the West recorded uninterrupted economic growth that was without any historical precedence. 'We are all Keynesians now', was the view shared by most worldly philosophers, at least till one arrives at the Thatcher-Reagan years of the early 1980s."

Later in the 80s, there was a phase where output levels were stagnant, yet price levels were going up in the US. Economists describe this as Stagflation (a combination of Stagnancy and Inflation). As Pulin B. Nayak phrased it, the Keynesian prescription could not provide any "magic solutions" to it.

Nayak further points out that around this time the Soviet Union too started to show its cracks leading to its collapse in the early '90s. The Soviet State with its centralised planning and all-pervasive command of the economy was gone. This too made the Keynesian prescription of State intervention seem less attractive. Free operation of the market system seemed more attractive. In many countries, including India, there was Liberalisation, that is, less of government rules and regulations and Privatisation, more of private sector activity.

But the recent financial crisis has "bust the myth of a self-regulating market". The US House and Senate have agreed on a $780 billion Economic Stimulus Bill to revive the sagging economy.

This shows that "Keynes had a point" .The State has to step in periodically to regulate the working of the market system.

GOI and RBI:

What are they Doing?

In the last few months the Government of India and the Reserve Bank of India had taken some steps to boost economic development.

For making ways for easing housing, auto and commercial loan rates, the RBI announced steps to pump in an estimated Rs 85,000 crore in the financial system by reducing deposit requirements and key rates. In November 2008, RBI reduced the mandatory Cash Reserve Ratio (CRR) and Statutory Liquidity Requirement (SLR) for banks by one per cent, besides lowering the rate at which it lends short-term funds to banks by 50 basis points (0.5%).

The Finance Ministry made certain changes in duties to help out the aviation and steel industry. The government also reduced export duty on certain iron and steel items in order to help out the steel and iron industry facing a fall in demand.

In December 2008, the Government announced Rs 20,000 crore stimulus package for the economy and provided additional funding, specifically for slumping sectors like power, exports, housing, auto, small and medium industries and infrastructure.

On 2nd January 2009, the Government has decided to inject Rs 100000 crore into the economy in association with the private sector. It intends to perk up specific sectors such as real estate and the infrastructure sector.

If the government will inject these money into long-term projects like airports, universities, school-colleges, low income housing, infrastructure, irrigation etc., it will drive the economy to long-term gains

Highlights of India's fiscal stimulus package December 7th, 2008

The following are the highlights of the fiscal stimulus package unveiled by the government to contain the impact of global financial crisis on the Indian economy:-

- Plan, non-plan expenditure of Rs.300,000 crore (Rs.3,000 billion/$60 billion) in four months
- Parliament nod to be sought for Rs.20,000 crore more toward plan expenditure
- Across-the-board cut of four percent in the ad valorem central value-added tax
- Interest subvention of two percent on export credit for labour intensive sectors
- Additional allocations for export incentive schemes
- Full refund of service tax paid by exporters to foreign agents
- Incentives for loans on housing for up to Rs.500,000 and up to Rs.2 million
- Limits under the credit guarantee scheme for small enterprises doubled
- Lock-in period for loans to small firms under credit guarantee scheme reduced
- India Infrastructure Finance Co allowed to raise Rs.100 billion through tax-free bonds
- Norms for government departments to replace vehicles relaxed

- Import duty on *naphtha* for use by the power sector is being reduced to zero
- Export duty on iron ore fines eliminated
- Export duty on lumps for steel industry reduced to five percent

Planning Commission's Deputy Chairman comments

"India's fiscal deficit will be much higher than anticipated this fiscal", Planning Commission Deputy Chairman Montek Singh Ahluwalia said after the Rs.3,000-billion fiscal stimulus announcement by Prime Minister Manmohan Singh. "The fiscal deficit will be higher than what was expected to be. We don't have the numbers as of now, though, they will come once they are calculated again," Ahluwalia told reporters.

He, however, noted that the Indian economy is in a better shape than many countries.

Dwelling on the Rs.3,000-billion fiscal stimulus announced by Prime Minister Manmohan Singh Sunday, Ahluwalia said: "The stimulus package has been announced to minimise the effect of the global slowdown on the Indian economy."

"Significant steps have also been taken for boosting the housing sector," he said.

The Reserve Bank of India (RBI) announced it would shortly put in place a refinance facility of Rs.40 billion (Rs.4,000 crore) for the National Housing Bank, the state-owned principal agency, to promote housing finance institutions.

RBI also said that in addition, one of the areas where plan expenditure can be increased relatively easily is the Indira Awas Yojana, a government-sponsored initiative to promote rural housing for people living below the poverty line.

As a further measure of support for this sector, state-run banks will soon announce a package for borrowers of home loans in two categories: up to Rs.500,000 and between Rs.500,000 and Rs.2 million.

Ahluwalia said the monetary steps have sent a message to banks that they need to lower the interest rates. "The message has already gone. It may take some time for the system to respond but the rates will come down."

According to him, the government was looking at additional spending in core sector and would try to spend what has already been budgeted.

"We are also taking steps to ensure bank lending to industry," he added, and added that a 'supportive environment' was needed for core sector financing.

"We expect the companies to pass on the benefit of tax cut to the consumers. However, the market forces will ensure the companies pass on the benefits of tax cuts to the consumers," Ahluwalia said.

"Today, the major concern of the infrastructure sector is financing, the government is trying to extend financial support to the infrastructure projects through financing," he said.

"Indian infrastructure finance companies are being given permission to mobilise up to Rs.10,000 crore (Rs.100 billion) through tax-free bonds. This amount will be used to fund infrastructure projects," he said.

Finance Secretary Comments

According to Finance Secretary, Arun Ramanathan, the impact of the four percent cut in central VAT would be Rs.8,700 crore (Rs.87 billion/$1.75 billion).

Highlights of the second stimulus package, January 29, 2009 -

The package which sought to lower down the impact of global slowdown on various sectors, with entailing a loss of Rs 8700 crore, in the remaining four months of 2008-09 , aims to revive sectors like housing, exports, automobile, textiles and small and medium enterprises (SMEs).

The highlights of the package were as follows:

• Package includes, the CENVAT on all products - except non petroleum goods - have been reduced from 14, 12, and 8 % to 10, 8 and 4% for various categories. (CENVAT is Central Value Added Tax, replacement of earlier MODVAT)

• Full exemption from basic customs duty has been effected on naphtha to provide relief to the power sector.

• With the implementation of the package the export duty on iron ore fines has been withdrawn, the levy on export of iron lumps has been cut from 15 to 5 per cent.

• Government seeks to provide relief to the housing sector with public sector banks will shortly announce a package for borrowers of home loans in two categories: up to 500,000 rupees and 500,000 rupees to 2 million rupees.

• For small and micro enterprises, the limits under the credit guarantee scheme have been doubled to 10 million rupees. The lock-in period for loans covered under the existing credit guarantee scheme is also being reduced from 24 to 18 months to encourage banks to extend more loans under the scheme.

• In an incentive for the automobile sector, government departments are also being allowed to replace older vehicles within the allowed budget, in relaxation of extant economy instructions.

Others

Realty sector majors like DLF and UNITECH, particularly in the non-metros felt that the package would boost demand for houses.

But the auto industry is disappointed at being excluded from the list of industries that are covered by the package. The stimulus 2.0 package has announced that the PSU banks are likely to provide a line of credit to NBFCs for purchase of commercial vehicles. Also an accelerated depreciation of 50 per cent was supposed to be provided for commercial vehicles to be purchased between January 1 and March 31, 2009.

As a one-time measure, states will be given support to purchase buses for their urban transport systems. The package has somewhat overlooked the liquidity crisis being faced by the auto component industry amongst whom a majority who are exporters are suffering from the lack of line of credit.

The Interim Budget

On 16 February 2009, Minister of External Affairs, Mr Pranab Mukherjee, as in- charge for Finance Ministry, announced the Pre-Election Interim Budget 2009 for the Fiscal 2009-10.

He announced nothing except his appraisal of the Government's performance in the last 5 years. Markets and the corporate world had anticipated lot of changes and reframing of policies to weather the current global economic downturn however, the Interim Budget said hardly anything on that matter.

Mr Pranab Mukherjee has however pointed out that the major policy announcement would take place after the General Elections in the Regular announcement of the General Budget to be held in June, 2009.

Highlights of the Interim Budget 2009-10:

- The Gross Domestic Product increased by 7.5 per cent, 9.5 per cent, 9.7 percent and 9 per cent in the first four years from fiscal year 2004-05 to 2007-08, recording a sustained growth of over 9 per cent for three consecutive years for the first time. The growth drivers for the period were agriculture, services, manufacturing, along with trade and construction.

• Fiscal deficit down from 4.5 per cent in 2003-04 to 2.7 per cent in 2007-08 and Revenue deficit from 3.6 per cent to 1.1 per cent in 2007-08.

•The domestic investment rate as a proportion of GDP increased from 27.6 per cent in 2003-04 to 39 per cent in 2007-08. Gross Domestic savings rate shot up from 29.8 per cent to 37.7 per cent during this period.

• The Gross capital formation in agriculture as a proportion of agriculture GDP increased from 11.1 per cent in 2003-04 to 14.2 per cent in 2007-08.

• The tax to GDP ratio increased from 9.2 per cent in 2003-04 to 12.5 per cent in 2007-08.

• Annual growth rate of agriculture rose to 3.7 per cent during 2003-04 to 2007-08. The food grain production recorded an increase of 10 million tonnes each year during this period and touched an all time high of 230 million tonnes in 2007-08.

• While manufacturing sector recorded growth of 9.5 per cent per annum in the period 2004-05 to 2007-08, communication and construction sectors grew at the rate of 26 per cent and 13.5 per cent per annum respectively.

• Exports grew at an annual average growth rate of 26.4 per cent in US dollar terms in the period 2004-05 to 2007-08. Foreign trade increased from 23.7 per cent of GDP in 2003-04 to 35.5 per cent in 2007-08.

Outlook for The Year 2009

• Despite the global financial crisis which began in 2007 impacting most emerging market economies, 7.1 per cent rate of GDP growth in the current year makes India the second fastest growing economy in the world.

- Fallout of global slowdown on Indian economy were countered with fiscal stimulus packages announced on December 7, 2008 and January 2, 2009 providing tax relief to boost demand and increasing expenditure on public projects.

- Government accorded approval to 37 infrastructure projects, worth Rs 70,000 crore from August, 2008 to January, 2009 alone.

- Under PPP mode, 54 Central Sector infrastructure projects with a project cost of Rs 67,700 crore given in-principal or final approval and 23 projects amounting to Rs 27,900 crore approved for viability gap funding in 2008-09.

- India Infrastructure Finance Company Ltd. (IIFCL) to refinance up to 60 per cent of commercial bank loans for PPP projects involving total investment of Rs 1,00,000 crore in infrastructure over the next eighteen months.

- In addition to RBI taking number of monetary easing and liquidity enhancing measures such as reduction in cash reserve ratio, statutory liquidity ratio and key policy rates, Government has taken specific measures which include extension of export credit for labour intensive exports, improving pre and post shipment credit availability, additional allocations for refund of Terminal Excise Duty/CST and export incentive schemes besides removal of export duty and export ban on certain items. A Committee of Secretaries set up to address procedural problems faced by exporters.

- Record US $32.4 billion FDI received in 2007-08 and notwithstanding financial uncertainty and slowdown, FDI inflows during April-November, 2008 were US $23.3 billion recording a growth of 45 per cent over the same period in 2007.

Observations

The total cost of subsidies (including bonds) and other packages is Rs. 223,525 Crores ($45.9 Billion) which means, then it works out to 4.4% of the India's GDP. If the Government adds the reduction in tax collections, it could cost 1 per cent of GDP. According to the Economic Advisory Council (EAC), the Fiscal Deficit in the Union Budget had been placed at 2.5%, the addition of 4.4% and 1% to this number would definitely raise the total to nearly 8% of the GDP. Credit Rating agencies like Standard & Poor's (S & P), Moody's and Fitch are closely watching India's fiscal shortfall and this would definitely force them to downgrade India's Sovereign Debt rating. On Tue, Feb 24, 2009 S & P has reaffirmed India's rating to BBB, means downgrading India from "Stable" to "Negative" outlook.

India's Fiscal Deficit swells to 8 per cent of the annual gross domestic product, government spending likely to rise and tax rate cut are less likely. On negative outlook, Standard & Poor's has changed India's outlook to negative from stable and assigned BBB- Sovereign Rating. However, Government has reduced Excise Duty and Service Tax to shore-up the economy.

What would happen, if the Fiscal Deficit rises? It means that the Government will borrow extra to finance their expenditures (planned or non-planned). We won't evade the higher monetary inflation. If the Government borrows extra for its spending, then the level of money supply will rise because it will force the Reserve Bank of India (RBI) to print more money – which would lead to the higher inflation at least in the medium term. Currently, India's national debt is 59% of the annual gross domestic product (Central and State Government combined). Maybe the short-term Government borrowing will prevent the further fall in inflation. There is also a possibility of higher interest rates in the long run.

As a result, there is a limited room for the Government to ramp up the spending without causing the structural harm to the economy. That's why the Government is reluctant to cut tax rates and in the near future, Government may also consider reducing subsidy burden on Oil and Fertiliser by 1.6% of the GDP and this Interim Budget proves merely a performance review of the Government. Government has admitted that the worst is yet to come and the painful time ahead.

Omkar Goswami comments

Omkar Goswami, chairman of CERG Advisory, sarcastically observes that the fiscal deficit has gone through the roof. By its own admission, the central government's fiscal deficit for 2008-09 will be 6 per cent of GDP — up from 2.7 per cent in 2007-08. Add an extra 1.8 per cent on account of 'special securities' issued by the Centre to additionally subsidise fertilisers and oil, and another 3.5 per cent as the combined deficit of the states, and we are staring at a consolidated fiscal deficit of 11.3 per cent. I will bet that when the actual data arrives, the consolidated fiscal deficit for 2008-09 will cross 12 per cent of GDP.

Being economists, Manmohan Singh and P. Chidambaram must be upset at this high deficit. Chidambaram had worked tirelessly at bringing down the central government's above-the-line fiscal deficit from almost 5 per cent of GDP in 2003-04 to 2.7 per cent in 2007-08. He must be wincing at it shooting up to 6 per cent — plus an extra 1.8 per cent on account of below-the-line items.

According to Omkar Goswami, the previous 2008-09 budget had been 'mega-Keynesian' and based on the presumption : that GDP growth would not slow down; that huge expenditure outlays and loan relief would further stimulate domestic demand; and that excise relief would ignite further growth of manufacturing.

With things not working out that way, the budget came 'unstuck'. With falling growth, lower than expected revenue receipts, and way higher than budgeted expenditure, especially on account of non-plan items such as burgeoning food and fuel subsidies, the cash deficit ballooned to 6 per cent of GDP instead of the budgeted 2.5 per cent.

Omkar Goswami warns: Do not think of this as the cost of kick-starting the economy through the two stimulus packages of

December 2008 and January 2009. Those will not account for an extra 1.5 percentage points of GDP. It is all about the growth bet going horribly wrong, and along with it the assumptions regarding the buoyancy of tax revenues. The 2008-09 Budget had precious little room for manoeuvre. India had to achieve at least 8.5 per cent GDP growth and deliver around 20 per cent increase in revenues for the deficit to be around 2.5 per cent. It has not happened. And nobody dared pull the plug on spending. Indeed, John Maynard Keynes was invoked by all and sundry based on a facile assumption that we could spend our way out of trouble, irrespective of what we spent it on.

Where now? I am afraid that we are in very dangerous territory. With the combined deficit set to breach 12 per cent of GDP, we are looking at a heavy borrowing plan that will put upward pressure on interest rates — forcing the Reserve Bank's hands to further cut the repo rate and the CRR. We are also looking at under 7 per cent GDP growth in 2008-09, and probably 6 per cent growth the next year. And a very unruly, fractured coalition government. So, all the good work done by Chidambaram has been wrecked by electoral profligacy. And will remain wrecked for the next couple of years, as spending your way out of trouble carries more dangers than realised. And because diabetics should never be allowed to keep their hands in the cookie jar.

Comments of the CPI-M

The Communist Party of India-Marxist (CPI-M) said that the measures would fail to stimulate the economy. "The stimulus package is grossly inadequate to meet the impact of the global crisis".

"There is only a mention of the meagre Rs.20,000 crore (Rs.200 billion) - less than 0.5 percent of India's GDP - additional plan outlay announced on Dec 7, 2008, and no further spending plan has been announced. What is required is a comprehensive debt-relief package for the state governments and real transfer of resources from the centre to the states," the CPI-M politburo said.

By ruling out any further increase in public investment in the current financial year and announcing that further fiscal measures will only be contained in the annual plan for the next fiscal, the United Progressive Alliance government is shifting the burden on to the next government, the CPI-M said.

Amartya Sen and Bimal Jalan on the Recession and government efforts

Amartya Sen has asked the Manmohan Singh government to be careful, but also said that the governments of India, China and Brazil can take up "a lot of initiatives" that will not only protect them, but also help in speedy recovery of the global economy.

Bimal Jalan, former Governor of the Reserve Bank of India and Rajya Sabha member, refused to make a forecast on economic growth this year or the next. But he did confess that, he might have expected 5 to 7 per cent growth in year 2009.

Now he has downgraded it to 4 to 6 per cent, saying he would be surprised if it settles outside that range. He said that he has changed his view because of overseas developments, and because the recession is deeper and more widespread than was anticipated a month or two ago.

When told that his new range could mean close to zero growth in the second half of the year (since growth in the first half was 7.8 per cent), he does not flinch from the possibility, though he argues that it will not be a depression.

With that pessimistic scenario in view, he says: The cardinal lesson is that you must take anticipatory action. And when it is a short-term loss of confidence, then you must do more than what is needed on the basis of technical reasoning. Also, don't go by what other countries are doing, do what works best in your own country.

Asked to elaborate on that last point, he says India has a large number of poor people, whose consumption basket comprises essentials, whereas government duties are on non-essentials.

Therefore, cutting taxes to reduce prices does not help the poor. It may not even lead to increased demand for other goods, because people are scared of losing their jobs. In short, he is not in favour of tax cuts as a solution.

So does he think the government should be spending more? Yes he does, but he agrees that the governance and government capability are such that governments are unable to spend the money that they are given.

If the government should be doing more than is technically needed, does he think that the fiscal deficit should be taken even higher than the likely figure of 7 per cent for this year, including off-balance sheet items? Yes, he says emphatically, though how that is to be done is not clear, if greater spending is not feasible and tax giveaways are not advisable.

Asked to comment on what the government and Reserve Bank of India (RBI) have done so far in response to the downturn, and whether the monetary authority responded late to the downturn, Jalan says he will not criticise the RBI.

I don't want to point fingers. I am a policy person, they have taken a number of small steps, but their sum total has not solved the problem. Now they are thinking of a second dose. So it remains self-evident that what they have done is not enough. Partly, he says, this is because no one knows the extent of the problem. The issues keep changing every day.

Asked how long he thinks the downturn will last, and whether it will go beyond 2009, he does not answer directly. No one anticipated the severity of the international meltdown. I would not bet against a third year of recession.

But he concedes that it is logical to expect a bit of an upturn by the fourth calendar quarter of 2009 by which time the monetary easing will have begun to take effect, and a low base effect would also kick in. Also, by then the US recession would have been twice as long as the average post-War recession.

Reverting to the issue of whether the government has handled the situation well or badly, he argues that the issue is not what you did in 2008, it is what you did not do in 2007. We are paying for yesterday's exuberance. The argument is that if stock market excess and the asset price bubble had been tackled earlier, then the pain now would have been less.

There was a lot of corporate excess last year; they were buying companies at home, companies abroad. Companies were over-leveraged because of excessive optimism and policy was myopic.

He contends that RBI had seen the excessive exuberance and indicated that it may not last. When the cycle was on an excessive upswing, we should have put sand in the wheels.

Finally, asked to comment on whether India should integrate with the world economy, he answers emphatically in the affirmative. The results are there to see, integration has benefited the economy.

But on financial integration, he is more cautious. You should be open to the extent that you can use those funds. Don't open up in such a manner that someone investing in dollars gets an 80 per cent return on the stock market, which is what some FIIs got.

Some other comments on Government Role

In a TV interview (on CNBC-TV 18, Feb 25, 2009) Dr. Subir Gokarn, Chief Economist : Asia-Pacific, S and P, said that the government's recently-announced stimulus package (Rs 30,000 crore additional stimulus) may not be justified. He called it "an unwarranted kind of stimulus", "a rather risky move and it has an immediate impact on deficit without the corresponding impact on demand."

To quote, "It will immediately impact the deficit and tax collections will go down without having the kind of certainty or assurance that people are going to actually start to spend money. For example, one won't buy a house because he doesn't get finance. All of the excise concessions on cement, etc. are not going to have an impact. So this is a rather risky move and it has an immediate impact on deficit without the corresponding impact on demand. Hence it is really quite, perhaps, an unwarranted kind of a stimulus."

Ajit Ranade, Chief Economist, Aditya Birla Group, does not share Gokarn's view. "I disagree with Gokarn that it cannot have any impact on demand but I think it will have some effect even though housing demand will depend on many other things including interest rates. There is a lot of pipeline investment being planned and certainly the excise concessions will help."

RBI Announcement

On 2 March 2009 the Reserve Bank announced further fiscal stimulus. Here is the text of the announcement made by its Chief General Manager, Alpana Killawala (Press Release: 2008-2009/1432):

Since the release of the Reserve Bank's Third Quarter Review on January 27, 2009, the global financial and economic conditions have further deteriorated as revealed by the latest available information. The US real GDP contracted sharply at an annualised rate of 6.2 per cent in the fourth quarter of 2008 and the unemployment rate in the US has moved up to 7.6 per cent. The real GDP in the euro area has also declined by 1.5 per cent in the fourth quarter of 2008. Reflecting deteriorating global demand, Japanese exports fell by 45.7 per cent (y-o-y) in January 2009. The Japanese economy also contracted sharply by 3.3 per cent in the fourth quarter of 2008. The fourth quarter real GDP numbers of several advanced economies have turned out to be worse than expected. The uncertainty, therefore, on global recovery has increased.

As a response, the governments all over the world continue to unveil expansionary fiscal policies. Central banks have also taken several measures to stimulate demand and moderate the impact of the global downturn and credit crunch on their economies. The

US Fed and the Bank of Japan have increased quantitative and credit easing measures. The UK further reduced its policy rate by 50 basis points to 1.0 per cent. Among emerging market economies (EMEs), Korea, Indonesia, Thailand, Chile and Mexico reduced their policy rates.

India's financial sector continues to be resilient in the face of global financial turmoil. Our financial markets continue to function in an orderly manner. India's growth trajectory has, however, been impacted both by the financial crisis and the follow-on of global economic downturn. This impact has turned out to be deeper and wider than anticipated earlier. Concurrently, because of global developments coupled with supply and demand management measures at home, inflation is on the decline along the expectations of the Third Quarter Review.

Reflecting these developments, the aim of various measures initiated by the Reserve Bank since mid-September 2008 has been to augment domestic and forex liquidity and to ensure that credit continues to flow to productive sectors of the economy. Notably, since mid-September 2008, the Reserve Bank has reduced the repo rate under the Liquidity Adjustment Facility (LAF) from 9.0 per cent to 5.5 per cent, reduced the reverse repo rate under the LAF from 6.0 per cent to 4.0 per cent, the Cash Reserve Ratio (CRR) from 9.0 per cent to 5.0 per cent of Net Demand and Time Liabilities (NDTL) and the Statutory Liquidity Ratio (SLR) from 25.0 per cent to 24.0 per cent of NDTL.

The cumulative amount of actual or potential primary liquidity made available to the financial system through various measures initiated by the Reserve Bank is over Rs. 3,88,000 crore. Besides, the reduction in SLR by one percentage point of NDTL has made available liquid funds of the order of Rs.40,000 crore for the purpose of credit expansion. This sizeable easing has ensured a comfortable liquidity position. The overnight money market rate has remained near or below the lower bound of the LAF corridor since November 3, 2008.

Consequent to the announcement of fiscal stimulus packages, the market borrowing programme of the Central Government for

2008-09 was raised to Rs.3,42,769 crore (gross) and Rs.2,66,539 crore (net) as against the budgeted amount of Rs.1,76,453 crore (gross) and Rs.99,000 crore (net). Against this enhanced borrowing programme, market borrowing of the Central Government has been Rs.2,66,276 crore (gross) and Rs.1,92,315 crore (net) up to March 3, 2009. In terms of the amendment to the Memorandum of Understanding on Market Stabilisation Scheme (MSS) on February 26, 2009, an amount of Rs. 45,000 crore will be transferred in installments from the MSS cash account to the normal cash account of the Government of India by March 31, 2009. An equivalent amount of government securities issued under the MSS would now form part of the normal market borrowing of the Government of India. This arrangement should provide comfort to the market. Furthermore, the Reserve Bank has also conducted purchase of government securities under its Open Market Operations (OMO). Such operations will be conducted as warranted by evolving monetary and financial market conditions.

The yield on the 10-year benchmark government securities, which hardened from 5.87 per cent on January 23, 2009 to 6.43 per cent on January 30, 2009, has since softened to 6.04 per cent on March 3, 2009. Taking the signal from the reductions in the repo and reverse repo rates in recent months, all public sector banks and several private sector and foreign banks have reduced their benchmark prime lending rates (BPLRs). Since the announcement of the Third Quarter Review, eleven banks have cut their BPLRs ranging from 25 basis points to 125 basis points. Several banks have also cut their deposit interest rates.

The Reserve Bank has been constantly monitoring global developments along with the domestic economic situation. On the positive side, inflationary pressures have eased significantly. Inflation as measured by year-on-year variations in the Wholesale Price Index (WPI) has declined to 3.36 per cent as on February 14, 2009, down by about three-fourths from the high of 12.91 per cent as on August 2, 2008. However, consumer price inflation, as reflected in various consumer price indices, is in the range of 9.85-11.62 per cent as of December 2008-January 2009, has yet to show moderation. Consumer price inflation has remained at elevated level due to increase in primary articles prices. With WPI inflation having moderated significantly, consumer price inflation may also be expected to decline, though with a lag.

At the same time, there is evidence of further slowing down of economic activity. Exports registered negative growth for the four recent consecutive months, October 2008-January 2009. Overall exports growth during 2008-09 (April-January) at 13.2 per cent was significantly lower than 24.2 per cent during the same period of the last year. The Index of Industrial Production (IIP) registered a negative growth of 2.0 per cent during December 2008, with the manufacturing sector returning a negative growth of 2.5 per cent. IIP growth during April-December 2008 at 3.2 per cent was about one-third of 9.0 per cent during the corresponding period of the previous year due to slowdown in all the major sectors. Real GDP growth in the third quarter of 2008-09 (September-December 2008) has been placed at 5.3 per cent by the Central Statistical Organisation (CSO). The services sector, which has been the main engine of growth during the last several years, has also been slowing down. Business confidence has been dented significantly and investment demand has decelerated.

Non-food bank credit growth reached a peak of 29.4 per cent (Rs.5,82,344 crore) on a year-on-year basis as on October 10, 2008 as compared with 23.3 per cent (Rs. 3,74,054 crore) as on October 12, 2007. Subsequently, year-on-year non-food bank credit growth decelerated to 24.3 per cent as on December 19, 2008, as credit expansion during the period between October 10, 2008 and December 19, 2008 at Rs. 30,889 crore was much lower as compared with Rs. 1,05,774 crore during the corresponding period of the previous year. According to the latest data, non-food bank credit has decelerated further to 19.7 per cent (y-o-y) as on February 13, 2009 as compared with 22.7 per cent as on February 15, 2008 as credit expansion during the period between December 19, 2008 and February 13, 2009 at Rs. 8,091 crore was sharply lower than that of Rs. 86,978 crore in the corresponding period of the last year. At this level, non-food bank credit expansion remains below the indicative projection of 24.0 per cent in the Third

Quarter Review of the Monetary Policy. The total flow of resources to the commercial sector from banks and non-banks during 2008-09 so far (up to February 13, 2009) at Rs.4,98,136 crore was lower than Rs.6,08,351 crore during the corresponding period of the last year.

Even as some public sector and private sector banks have cut lending rates in response to the Reserve Bank's monetary policy stance, concerns over rising credit risk together with the slowing of economic activity appear to have moderated credit growth. The Reserve Bank continues to urge banks to monitor their loan portfolio and take early action, to prevent asset impairment down the road and safeguard the gains of the last several years in improving asset quality. At the same time, banks should price risk appropriately and ensure that creditworthy enterprises continue to get funding.

On a review of the current global and domestic macroeconomic situation, the Reserve Bank has decided to take the following further measures:

Repo Rate

- To reduce the repo rate under the liquidity adjustment facility (LAF) by 50 basis points from 5.5 per cent to 5.0 per cent with immediate effect.

Reverse Repo Rate

- To reduce the reverse repo rate under the LAF by 50 basis points from 4.0 per cent to 3.5 per cent with immediate effect.

It is expected that the reduction in the policy interest rates will further encourage banks to provide credit for productive purposes at viable interest rates. The Reserve Bank on its part would continue to maintain ample liquidity in the system.

Chidambaram's comments

As reported on the Business Standard, Home Minister P. Chidambaram on 6 March 2009 said that the country's economy was expected to show an upturn by third or fourth quarter of 2009-10 and register a 9 per cent growth by 2011.

While the economy is projected to expand by 7.1 per cent this year (2008-09), the third quarter gross domestic product growth is estimated at 5.3 per cent. This would mean that the economy has to grow by 7.6-7.7 per cent during January-March, Chidambaram said, adding that it was something that looked difficult.

The minister was speaking at a conference organised by the International Bar Association. "Even until about two-three months ago, we were pretty confident that we will navigate this difficult year and end with a growth of a little over 7 per cent. In the first half of the current fiscal year, growth was 7.8 per cent. We were hoping that in the second half we will do 6.5 per cent. But the results of our third quarter GDP growth have been quite depressing," he said.

Blaming the Western economies for weak regulation and being the originators of global economic crisis, Chidambaram said that regulations must always remain a step ahead of innovation. "The developed world has failed to live up to what it used to teach developing economies. Unless they set their house in order, the shadow of their failure will fall upon us and hurt us badly. The reward system in developed economies has become skewed and perverse," said Chidambaram.

The former finance minister outlined six points or crucial steps needed to bring the economy back on the growth track. The first being encouraging people to save more. India's current savings rate is at 35 per cent of its GDP. Boosting public investment in infrastructure, pruning government expenditure, stimulating domestic consumption and exports were the other focus areas identified by Chidambaram.

He admitted that India's fiscal deficit would be well above 6 per cent and pegged the revenue deficit at 5 per cent.

Talking about privatisation, Chidambaram said that it is a very restrictive ideology. "There is merit in having some public sector banks, insurance companies, oil firms and others so that there is a fair competition between public and private sectors," said Chidambaram.

IN BLACK AND WHITE

As the TIME magazine reported, if one visits the luxury stores in New Delhi, one finds no trace of the recession.

"The rest of the world might be absorbed by a global financial crisis, but you wouldn't know it here among the caramel coloured leather, hand printed silk scarves and blue Birkin bags."(TIME on World, 28 October 2008). Delhi seems to be untouched by the global recession .

This is partly because Delhi is surrounded by a prosperous farming and manufacturing belt that is not dependent on the financial services sector affected by the recession.

But more seriously it is because in Delhi as well as much of the rest of India, in stores, as well as in real estate, much of the buying and selling is done in Cash (rather than Credit). This means the credit crunch is a non-issue for it.

Also, one reason for the US facing sub-prime crisis and bank failure is that there most of the money involved was White. But in India (and China) almost 40 % of transactions are made in Black. It is the Parallel Economy using Black Money that drives the luxury market, and it is relatively immune to the recession, says TIME.

Black Money is considered evil and that is why it is called Black. But in the present crisis it may be a saviour. Black Money may stabilise the economy as it is facing the global downswing.

But what is Black Money?
What does Parallel Economy mean?

Black money is money that is generated by activities that are kept secret and these are not reported to the authorities. As such, this money is also not accounted to the fiscal authorities i.e., taxes are not paid on this money. White money, or simply Money, is what is shown in relevant accounts and on which due tax is paid.

There functions in some countries an unsanctioned sector in the economy whose objectives run parallel or side by side with the legitimate economy with its declared socio-economic objectives. This is variously termed as `parallel economy', 'black economy', 'unaccounted economy', 'illegal economy', 'subterranean economy', or 'unsanctioned economy'.

The amount of Black Money in India is mind-boggling. In India, the National Institute of Public Finance Policy (NIPFP) has estimated that the sum involved is as much as about Rs 40,000 crores or around 20 per cent of the GDP.. There is every possibility that it may be much higher, going even up to 50 per cent of GDP. The annual rate of growth of black money is likely to be higher than the annual growth-rate of GDP.

How does Black Money affect the Indian economy?

• It misdirects the allocation of national resources. A part of black money is kept in a form that contributes little or nothing to productive activities.

• It worsens the income-distribution black activities. Honest tax-payers end up earning much less than small shopkeepers who are corrupt or petty clerks who take tips.

• It makes official estimates of National Income, Savings, etc. difficult and so hinders the framing and implementing of right government policies.

• Violating exchange regulations, it leads to transfer of funds from India to foreign countries through clandestine channels.

• It has to be supported by musclemen, touts and brokers to combat the forces of law and order. What is more, there are income tax advisers, or chartered accountants in the pay of black money operators. Liaison officers or contact-men too flourish, negotiating favours from top bureaucracy and political bosses through bribes of black money.

• It vitiates the political system. I need not tell you how our MLAs, MPs, Ministers, party bosses go about taking black money donations in the name of `party funds'.

How did Black money grow to such astounding proportions?

• Malpractices during the period of the Second World War, when usual supplies of industrial goods from the West were cut off were how Black Money was generated in India.

• Trading in permits, quotas and licenses under the regime of quotas and licenses that started in mid 50s with the 1956 Industrial Policy Resolution, and grew in strength till the Liberalisation of the 90s. Price and distribution controls without adequate machinery of distribution added to the problem.

• High Tax Rates, defective Tax structure, massive tax evasion, both Direct and Indirect Taxes have been responsible.

• Enforcement of tax laws is very weak due to widespread corruption.

• Donation to political parties were banned in 1968 so as to reduce the influence of big business on the electoral process.

What happened was that businessmen realised that all that they have to do now is to pay some of their black money to the party leaders so as to ensure that they get all their permits and exemptions.

• The growth of public sector undertakings after the mid-'50s meant large tenders being invited for the various works, These tenders were awarded by the bureaucracy in consultation with the political bosses. This too encouraged underhand deals and growth of black money.

• Restrictions on depreciation and other business expenses (advertisement, entertainment, guest houses, payment of perquisites to directors) made businessmen take the maximum advantage of these provisions but convert the remaining money by various clandestine devices; and use it on luxury living.

The Direct Taxes Enquiry Committee (Wanchoo Committee), 1971, had said : "It is, therefore, no exaggeration to say that black money is like a cancerous growth in the country's economy which, if not checked in time, is sure to lead to its ruination".

Black Money in the Present Scenario

• As pointed out earlier, the presence of Black Money in the system has also provided India with a sort of immunity against the global credit crunch. A lot of Black Money is liquid and people want to spend it quickly rather than hang on to it when it is losing value. Hence in Delhi the luxury spending has been going on. However, it is not as if there has been no effect felt there. The recession had arrived in India during the festival season. The upper-middle-class salaried executives who got less of Diwali bonuses did cut back as compared to, say, the earlier year. But those who went for conspicuous consumption as a status symbol have indulged in it all the more.

• This process may be aided by thousands of people discovering that because of computerisation and consequent extensive cross checking by the tax department, there is no safe place to hide black money. They are in a hurry to spend it and in doing so, are putting in liquidity into the system.

• Black money in India may actually help the Indian economy in this recession. When one buys a house in India, one pays 25 % in black and 75% in white. Out of that 75%, he may be taking a bank loan of 80-90%. So the bank exposure is about 60-70%, not more. Even if he defaults, the bank , unlike in the U.S., is reasonably secure. Thus the fact that black money is used in real estate deals in India may actually reduce the impact of the recession on banks. The guess is that in China and India 40% of transactions are done in black money and that protects the remaining 60% and prevents Collateral Damage. In metropolitan cities like Bangalore and Hyderabad, the majority of buyers in real estate were IT professionals, the real estate prices have fallen sharply. But in cities like Lucknow and Nagpur 80% of the money involved was black money, and there real estate prices have neither risen dramatically nor fallen drastically. So the government should actually allow some flow of black money in the economic system so as to stabilise it.

• According to others, if the government can get the black money in India back into the mainstream, it will act as a huge cash cushion. If we can again have a scheme like "declare your black money, pay 20% of it as tax", the resulting tax revenue can make up for the loss of liquidity we are having. Of course, here it has to be remembered that much of the black money lies in real estate and luxury cars, and are illiquid.

• There are those who believe that India has US $ 1.456 billion cash stashed away illegally in the Swiss Bank. It is 1.8 times its GDP, that is, almost double! The Swiss Banking Association (SBA) has itself said in 2006 that Indian nationals have the largest quantity of illegal money in the Swiss Bank. This is probably a bigger `drain' than the one that had happened in the British Raj. The U.S.A. is now seeking information from the United Bank of Switzerland (U.B.S.) about Americans clandestinely storing money there. Such money, if released, can really help the U.S. economy out of the doldrums. There is a strong suggestion that India should try to do the same. If somehow that stupendous amount can be brought back into India, it may help tremendously in her recovery process. However, there are three problems here. (a)The Swiss Bank has a policy of protecting the client's privacy and may not co-operate with the Indian Government. (b)The money in the Swiss Bank does not belong to the Indian government but to individuals. Unless that money can be proven to be illegally earned, the Indian government cannot really take it into the national exchequer and then spend it. (c) Corruption at various levels in the Government may prevent the money so released from being spent the right way, for the right purpose.

A DIFERENT VIEW

Let us take a break from mainstream Economics, and look at what Marx and Marxists have to say on the matter.

The term that Marx and the Marxists have for Depression and Recession is CRISIS. Crises are part and parcel of the capitalist system or `Mode of Production'.

According to Karl Marx, human societies go through a progression of systems or **Modes of Production**. At first there is **Primitive Communism**, where people have hardly any property and whatever they have, they share in common. There is hardly any hostility among the people about property and possessions, and this Mode of Production is called **Non-Antagonistic Mode of Production.**

But as time passes, people earn and acquire more property and within the society sections or `classes' begin to develop. One class begins to get all the property and the other loses all their independence and work under the other class for just the bare minimum of food and clothing and shelter. Such a Mode of Production is called **Slavery** and because there are two classes – one possessing almost everything and the other almost nothing, there is hostility or **antagonism**. With time, slaves begin to rebel. Cultivation of land becomes more organised. Control passes from kings with soldiers and weaponry to noblemen and gentlefolk with lots of land under them as their legal property.

There emerges the next Mode of Production, **Feudalism**. Here too, property – which at this historical stage is basically Land – is owned by one class – the landed gentry or noblemen. The other class serves them and so is known as Serf. Like Slavery, Feudalism too is a divided society, with one class dominating the other, that is an **Antagonistic** Mode of production. The Serfs do the actual work of labouring in the fields, but most of their production they have to give up to the landlords as a customary tribute. This in course of time makes one class of society prosperous and the other impoverished.

There was the prevalence of this Mode of Production in Europe till the middle of the 18th century.

Then this system broke down due to a variety of happenings in history.

Why did Feudalism break down?

- A series of mechanical inventions.
- Accumulation of savings in the hands of the propertied class – gentry as well as tradespeople.
- Sea-voyages to Asia, Africa and other parts of the world – conquests and colonisations.
- Discontent among serfs leading to many breaking away from rural areas to urban areas.

All this led to the French Revolution in France and the Industrial Revolution in England. Out of this conflict a new Mode of Production emerged **Capitalism**.

Capitalism is also an **Antagonistic** Mode of Production. Here it is not Land but Capital or accumulated savings that is the most important factor of production. It is the possession or legal ownership of capital that determines one's position or class in society. Production takes place in factories with the help of heavy machinery. Goods in mass are produced, that is, produced in great quantities or numbers and with the use of machines operated by workers on the principle of division of labour. Goods are sold for money in the market. Out of the sales revenue, the businessmen or owners of Capital pay Wages to the Workers, and keep the rest for themselves as Profit. The Workers, in fact, get much less than the worth of the hours of labour that they put in and it is this extra or surplus that goes to the Capitalists or businessmen as Profits. So there occurs exploitation in the system, with one. Small firms get bigger and bigger, more and more efficient and powerful, those that win in the competition among themselves, become more and more powerful class (Capitalists) benefiting at the expense of the other (Labourers). This system is thus again an Antagonistic one.

When the sense of exploitation becomes acute the labourers , as a class, revolt against the capitalists. Class-conflict builds into a social revolution. This does not occur in just one factory or area but in the whole country or even across the various conflicts. Also, because production is going on at a fast rate and on a mass-scale, there sometimes is too much of it, in relation to what the people can and want to buy. Then goods produced start to remain unsold, factory-owners have goods piling up in their store-rooms, and the rate of profit falling. They realise that they have to reduce production levels. Since the machines cannot be disposed off, they dispose off the other factor – the workers. Workers start getting sacked, and there is widespread unemployment. This adds to their sense of exploitation and provides another very strong force for breaking out in a **Revolution.** The system of Capitalism is destroyed – violently.

Now should emerge a whole new mode of production, **Socialism.** Here all property is socially owned. No individual owns any land or money or factory and has no one working under him. The State as the administrative representative of the society owns everything. So every citizen of the State also owns everything collectively (and nothing privately). Since there is no private ownership of property, there is no reason for comparison, envy and conflict. This is thus a Non-Antagonistic Mode of Production. Remember the Mode of Production that human society began with – Primitive Communism. That too was a Non-Antagonistic Mode of

Production. But several centuries have gone in the mean time. Both factors of production and methods of production have undergone vast changes - in quality as well as quantity. So though ownership of property once again becomes common - and this society is described as communistic, it is no longer primitive in character.

Thus through a series of class-conflicts, one mode of production turns into another and this progression in history was called Dialectical by Marx.

With this background, now let me tell you what Marx and the Marxists specifically say about Recessions and Depressions.

Remember that under capitalism, because goods are mass-produced, there develops a situation when their total demand falls short of their total supply, leading to mass unemployment. This is the very situation which mainstream Economics calls Recession/ Depression and Marx called it CRISIS.

What is more, Marx and some Marxists hold that such crises are bound to occur in the capitalist mode of production. Crises are inevitable so long as the system in the country is Capitalistic and will stop forever only if instead the country runs through centralised planning under a Socialistic system. Crisis is generated internally by capitalism and is therefore inevitable.

Even here, there are two types of theories. One set known as **Possibility theories** say that crises are not a necessary feature of Capitalism. Ups and downs in the country's activity level, Inflation and Depression/Recession, Boom and Bust, are possible in a capitalistic system but can be corrected by State activity. If the government of the country is willing and able to manage the gap between aggregate supply and aggregate demand, such gaps need not blow up into full-fledged crisis-situations. When small competitive firms grow bigger and bigger and become monopolies , charging any price they want, does the government step in and put checks on such monopolistic practices? When too low wages are being paid to workers, who are in no position to bargain for higher wages, does the government see to it that at least some sort of minimum wages are paid ? If these, and similar measures are taken by the government, then the crisis may be averted. This did happen in England in the early and middle of the 20th century. This is why there was no revolution there and capitalism continued to flourish. After the 1930s, Keynesian policies (Roosevelt's New Deal) worked the same way in the U.S.A.

But the set of theories known as **Necessity theories** say that such `crisis management' can stave off a revolution for the time being. In fact, time and time again, crises may be averted or controlled. But eventually, in the long run, it is bound to take place. A series of crises will be occurring and even though after every crisis there comes an upsurge, the upsurges will get weaker and weaker. Government may intervene and control the situation once, twice, and several times, but because the problem is internal to the very nature of the capitalist system, it will crop up again. No State intervention will be able to suppress it for ever. As long as the Mode of Production remains capitalist, crises are not only possible or likely but will occur inevitably, necessarily. The ultimate solution is an attack on the capitalist system itself – a revolution of the working / labour class against the capitalist class – resulting in a complete overthrow of capitalism itself. Marx himself should be put in this set of thinkers, though the other set – which thinks that crises are possible but not necessary – are also Marxist thinkers.

In this way of thinking, therefore, the current recession may resolve itself in a few months or years but another will occur again. It is a matter of time. There will a series of recessions/depressions as long as the system remains capitalistic.

So the recession that has started in the US in late 2007 and by early 2009 become a global phenomenon "will also be controlled through various public and private measures but after the usual upswing and boom following recession/depression, there will be sooner or later another recession/depression – and another and another – till there is an end to the system that dominates the globe today – capitalism." The ultimate cure of crisis is in the end of capitalism.

But that end is too far in the future. We have a problem at hand!

Even Marxist economists say that at present the policy should be of government intervention to stimulate aggregate demand. So says, for example, Prabhat Patnaik, Professor, JNU, and a noted Marxist.

A four-member high-power task force was announced on U.N. Day (24 October 2008) by the United Nations (U.N.) to recommend reforms of the global financial system. The task force is to be headed by Nobel Prize-winning economist Joseph Stiglitz and includes Professor Prabhat Patnaik. On the current financial turmoil, he has commented that though there was this widely held view that the world was experiencing a global financial crisis, in reality it was a recession which could not be tackled by merely injecting liquidity into the system. "What we need to do is to spur demand and simply lowering the interest rate is not sufficient to achieve this," he said.

Professor Patnaik said, "the governments must be proactive and adopt expansionary fiscal policies with sufficient capital controls to take care of fears about flight of capital." He was of the firm view that there was tremendous scope in the Third World for governments to adopt aggressive fiscal policies to augment the infrastructural and other shortfalls, increase welfare expenditure and inject demand into the system.

IN CLOSING

Over the past couple of months, the recession has been deepening in the United States of America. The impact of the sub-prime crisis along with a slowdown in mortgages has led to a significant lowering of growth figures. Since the United States dominates the global economy, the slowdown there has had an impact on most of the global economic variables.

For India, it could mean a further appreciation in the rupee vis-à-vis the US dollar and a darkening of business outlook for sectors dependent on US companies. The overall impact of a US slowdown on India would, however, be minimal as the factors driving growth here are more local in nature. Unlike the rest of Asia, India has a strong domestic demand and so any slowdown elsewhere in the world is likely to have a more quiet impact on India. Strong growth in domestic consumption and significant spending on infrastructure are the two pillars of India's growth story. Corporate India is also learning to master the art of efficient capital management, reduction in costs and delivery of value-added services to sustain profit margins.

According to the IMF (International Monetary Fund), world will be suffering even more this year. Global growth prediction for the year 2009 is as low as 2.2 per cent. Growth rate below 3 per cent signifies a global recession. In fact, the predictions for US, Europe and Japan are even gloomier with contracting economy and negative growth rate being the prime indicator of days ahead.

The figure is lower by more than 0.7 per cent, what IMF had predicted in October 2008. Growth in the emerging and developing countries is predicted to take place at the rate of 5.1 per cent in the year 2009 but that again is much less than the October forecast. In India, our economic experts are expecting growth rate of 6 to 7 per cent , which shows that we are still in a better position than other nations.

So, by and large the effects of economic turmoil of previous year will be severely felt this year as well. The global financial crisis has worsened the conditions of credit availability. Foreign direct investment (FDI), so important for a growing economy like India's , had started moving back in the year 2008 and this year, that is the trend that is likely to continue.

India is witnessing slow industrial growth and the output in some core industries have declined significantly. Sectors like construction, housing, automobiles, retail activity, textiles, commercial vehicles, finance, petrochemicals, steel are going through a painful downturn in terms of sales as well as profits. Since the last few months, exports have dropped by as much as 12 per cent. India's expected GDP growth rate of more than 7 per cent is under serious doubt because of the current circumstances.

This year is going to be one of the challenging years for world economy and India in terms of growth and development. However, steps have been taken by the Finance Ministry as well as the Reserve Bank of India in the form of stimulus packages and monetary steps. The rate cuts are of critical importance for easing the flow of money into the financial system. The fiscal packages are focused upon the revival of most of the affected sectors. Lower price of crude oil and lower inflation are two positive signs. However, we must be prepared for challenging times as conditions are likely to remain tough throughout 2009 .

But let us not forget that Home Minister P Chidambaram has said that the country's economy was expected to show an upturn by third or fourth quarter of 2009-10 and registering a 9 per cent growth by 2011.

E.H.Goldratt, the Israeli business thinker, described by Fortune magazine as a "guru to industry", has said in an interview to the TOI in end-February, that the Indian economy would rebound in 2 months. "The negative growth in the industrial production in India in December was because of fear of demand falling in the future and not because of a lack of demand." Even from the U.S.A., his own research has found no evidence of a big economic crisis.

In the IIMs, this year the international offers were low, But to take the example of IIM-Bangalore, although the recruitment process was more sedate this time, it had worked out satisfactorily. "We are relieved that all our students were able to land jobs despite tough market conditions and the fear that the global meltdown would affect it adversely," IIM-B director Pankaj Chandra declared. "We had more companies this time due to less offers from regular firms. In the absence of some reputed international firms like Lehman Brothers and others, we not only invited more companies for placements, but also extended the recruitment process by a week," IIM-B faculty member (placement) Sourav Mukherji said. As for IIM-Ahmedabad, its students have an alternate plan just in case things get rough. The new trend among IIM-students is to accept job offers but also have an enterprise running by the side (like, say, stock-trading on the website).

So it is a matter of resourcefulness combined with optimism.

In closing, let us keep our hopes alive for an **upturn by the year-end**. Hopes? How will hope help? What have hopes got to do with economics, you may say?

Depression /Recession is not just a matter of supply and demand, liquidity and credit. It is in the ultimate a matter of the mind or spirit. As Amartya Sen put it, the current recession had occurred because of a loss of **confidence** and Depression/Recession occurs basically because of this loss of confidence.

So the cure has got to be confidence; confidence itself.

We just have to be confident that this Recession will soon be over, and so it will. Keynes himself had said the same: it is the "animal spirits" in men that do not allow Depression to be a permanent state of affairs. People recover simply because they have the spirit to recover. So do economies.

And let us not forget our **own philosophy:**

Chakravat parivartantey sukhani cha duhkhani cha.

Joys and sorrows change like a moving wheel. There's Business Cycle for you, with Recession/Depression alternating with Recovery/Boom.

Now see why I called the book Recession Challenge, and not just Recession?

GLOSSARY

A

Ad valorem: A tax or duty that is levied as a fixed percentage of the price of one unit of output

Adjustable Mortgage Rate (ARM): A mortgage in which the interest rate is adjusted according to an index - monthly, semiannually or annually. Reflect changes in interest rate.

Aggregate Demand: Total demand in an economy, of all goods and services , coming from all the people and organisations.

Aggregate Supply: Total supply of all the goods and services produced in an economy by individuals as well as organisations.

B

Basis Point: A unit that measures the changes in interest rates and bond yields. One basis point is equal to 0.01 percent of yield. An increase of 2 percent would be change of 200 basis points.

Business Cycle: A recurring economic period that is characterised by changes in the state of the economy, including recessions, booms, expansions and recoveries. Also called Trade Cycle.

C

Capitalism: Economic system (or Mode of Production) in which the means of production are owned by private persons, and operated for profit and where investments, distribution, income, production and pricing of goods and services are predominantly determined through the operation of a free market.

Cash Reserve Ratio (CRR): A bank regulation that sets the minimum reserves each bank must hold to customer deposits and notes. These reserves are designed to satisfy withdrawal demands, and would normally be in the form of cash currency stored in a bank vault (vault cash) or with a central bank.

Collateral Debt Obligations (CDOs): Investment-graded security backed by a pool of bonds, loans and other assets. CDOs do not specialise in one type of debt but are often non-mortgage loans or bonds. They are unique because they represent different types of debt and credit risk (trenches or slices). Each slice has a different maturity or associated risk. The higher the risk, the more paying the CDO.

Conspicuous Consumption: Purchase of commodities not so much for their usefulness but for the purpose of showing off to others.

Credit: is the provision of resources (such as granting a loan) by one party (lender or creditor) to another party (borrower or debtor) where that second party does not reimburse the first party immediately, thereby generating a debt and instead arranges either to repay or return those resources (or material(s) of equal value) at a later date. It is thus a deferred payment.

Credit Crunch: Also known as a credit squeeze or credit crisis, is a reduction in the general availability of loans (or credit) or a sudden tightening of the conditions required to obtain a loan from the banks. A credit crunch generally involves a reduction in the availability of credit independent of a rise in official interest rates.

D

Deflation: Deflation is the opposite of inflation; a period of falling prices when the purchasing power of the money is rising. But it is usually the result of government policies.

Demand: Desire backed by purchasing power; depends on price of the product, price of related products, the income level of the buyer, his tastes. Can be understood in Micro as well as Macro concept. Unless specified, it is usually taken to be in the Micro sense. That is, demand for a specific good or service coming from a specific individual, household or organisation. When all the demands for all the goods and services coming from all the individuals and organisations in a country are taken together, it is Aggregate Demand.

Depression: A stage in a Business Cycle when there is a sharp as well as sustained decline in the activity level of the entire economy. A serious and severe form of recession, a depression is characterised by abnormal increases in unemployment, difficulty in credit, diminishing output and investment, numerous bankruptcies, reduced amounts of business, as well as highly volatile relative currency value fluctuations, mostly devaluations.

Dow Jones Industrial Average (Dow): Price Weighted average of 30 blue chip stocks that make up the Dow. Used by media to represent the overall price movement of the stocks on the New York Stock Exchange.

E

Exports: Goods sold to another country.

Excess Demand: Amount demanded that is not met by the supply in the market, can be understood in both Micro and Macro senses.

Excess Supply: Amount supplied to the market that is not absorbed by the demand coming to the market, can be understood as both Micro and Macro senses.

F

FMCG (Fast Moving Consumer Goods): Products sold quickly at relatively low cost. The absolute profit made on FMCG products is relatively small, but they generally sell in large quantities, so that the total profits on such products can be large. Examples of FMCG : toiletries, soap, cosmetics, teeth cleaning products, shaving products and detergents, as well as other non-durables such as glassware, light bulbs, batteries, paper products and plastic goods, pharmaceuticals, consumer electronics, packaged food products and drinks. FMCG products contrast with durable goods such as kitchen appliances, which are generally replaced less than once a year.

Federal Reserve: Known as the "Fed". It is made up of a board of governors appointed by the President of US that manages the Federal Reserve system of US and determines interest rates. Similar job is done by Reserve Bank of India in India.

Fiscal Policy: The government's policy relating to the budget (especially with government expenditure, taxation and borrowing). Fiscal Policy is Expansionary when government expenditure is increased and taxation reduced. It is Contractionary when government expenditure is curtailed and taxation made more stringent. The corresponding term is Monetary Policy.

Fix Rate Mortgage: A home mortgage in which the initial interest rate is fixed for the life of the loan and the monthly payments remain the same.

Forex: Abbreviation for Foreign Exchange.

G

Gross Domestic Product (GDP): The value of all final goods and services produced within the physical boundaries of a country within a year.

H

Hedge Fund: Largely unregulated and privately managed investment funds that use aggressive financial strategies which are prohibited to mutual funds. In other words Hedge fund is a collective investment, much like a unit trust or investments trust. The difference is that hedge fund managers aim to make money whether the market is moving up, down or sideways. They do this using a range of complicated specialist techniques.

I

Imports: Goods bought from another country.

Invoice: a document sent by supplier to customer, itemising the products supplied, their prices and the total amount of money owed; a request for payment.

Inflation: A phase of rising prices, when the general level of prices shows persistent and substantial rise. A corresponding opposite is Deflation.

Interest: a charge paid for borrowing money.

J

Junk Bond: High Risk bonds that pay interest rate well above market rates. Usually these are issued by lower rated companies.

L

Lay-Off: Temporary suspension or permanent termination of employment of an employee or (more commonly) a group of employees for business reasons, such as business slow-down or interruption in work.

Liquidity: The ability of an asset to be converted into cash quickly and without any price discount.

M

Macro Economics: A branch of economics that deals with the performance, structure, and behaviour of a national economy as a whole. Studies National Income, Employment, Aggregate Demand and Aggregate Supply, Money, Interest Rate, Inflation, Prices, etc. Associated with the name of Keynes, Tobin, Feldman, Lucas. Corresponding opposite: Micro-economics.

Micro Economics: Study of economic activity as it applies to individual firms or well-defined small groups of individuals or economic sectors. Micro economics investigate the concepts of production and specialisation using economic principles. Corresponding opposite: Macro-economics.

Money Market: Market for short-term debt instruments. In finance, the money market is the financial market for short-term borrowing and lending. It provides short-term liquid funding for the global/domestic financial system. Short-term debt instruments such as treasury bills, commercial papers, bankers' acceptances, and certificates of deposit are traded in the money market.

Monetary Policy: Policies of the government, central bank (Reserve Bank in India), or monetary authority of a country to controls (a) the supply of money, (b) availability of money and (c) cost of money or rate of interest. Corresponding term: Fiscal Policy.

Mortgage backed Securities (MBS): Bonds which are a general obligation of the issuing institution but are collateralised by a pool of mortgages. These securities are structured by pooling together standardised residential mortgage loans of similar characteristics. The investor purchases a pro-rata share of the interest and principal that the borrowers pay on the mortgage loans in the pool.

Mutual Fund: A professionally managed company of collective investments that collects money from many investors and puts it in stocks, bonds, short-term money market instruments, and/or other securities. It is an account established by a financial services company that combines the money of many people and invests it in a variety of financial instruments.

N

NASSCOM: A global trade organisation, with over 1200 members, of which over 250 are global companies from the United States, Europe, and Asia. NASSCOM's member companies are in the business of software development, software services, software products, IT-enabled/BPO services and e-commerce. NASSCOM was set up in 1988 to facilitate business and trade in software and services and to encourage advancement of research in software technology. It is a not-for-profit organisation, registered under the Indian Societies Act, 1860.Currently, NASSCOM is headquartered in New Delhi, India, with regional offices in the cities of Mumbai, Chennai, Hyderabad, Bangalore, Pune and Kolkata.

NEW DEAL: A set of plans and programmes that President Roosevelt initiated in U.S.A. between 1933 and 1938 with the goal of providing relief(work) to the unemployed, reform of business and financial practices.

P

Price Level: an average of the prices of all the commodities and services produced and sold in a country.

R

Recession: Downward or low phase of a Business Cycle, characterised by loss of jobs and output.

Repo Rate: The rate at which the banks can borrow money from a central bank of the country (Reserve Bank in India) in order to avoid scarcity of funds.

S

Sub-Prime: A type of loan or finance that is given to individuals with poor credit intention and capacity of such individuals are considered unsure.

Supply: Production or output brought to the market, to be sold at a price; both a Macro and Micro concept. Aggregate Supply is the total of all the goods and services that are supplied in a country by all its productive units – individuals and organisations.

T

Tariff: Tax imposed on imports so as to make it more expensive; also called import duty or customs duty.

Trade Cycle: Business Cycle.

U

Unemployment: Joblessness of those who are able and willing to work. People who offer themselves in the job market but are either unable to get jobs or thrown out of jobs. Unemployment may be of different types – rural, urban, open, disguised, and so on.

Unit Linked: Unitised insurance funds or unit-linked insurance funds are a form of collective investment offered through life assurance policies. These are investment vehicles in which the money of numerous investors are pooled together and the entire pool is used to purchase assets, i.e. equities, bonds.

V

VAT – Value Added Tax: an indirect tax applied to the value added to a product at any stage of the production or distribution change. MODVAT is a modified VAT and CENVAT is a centrally administered VAT.

W

Wage: Payment of workers or labourers; price of the labour as a factor of production.

God Does Not Play Dice

By David A. Shiang

Does God play dice with the universe?
Do events happen by chance?
Do we have free will?
Einstein right in his assessment of quantum theory?

If you seek answers to such questions, you have come to the right place. In my groundbreaking book **God Does Not Play Dice.**

- The final and only solution to the free will problem.
- Why Stephen Hawking is wrong when he says that there is 'evidence' that God plays dice.
- The role of memory in solving free will problem.
- The type of certainty that can be achieved.
- How past, present and future are interrelated.
- Why key ideas presented by Richard Dawkins and John Allen Paulos are false.
- the reason why much of our worrying is misplaced and irrelevant.

Noting and Drafting

By M.K. Agarwal

Basic note in a file is written by an Office Assistant/ Assistant Section Officer. A good note should properly define and analyse the problem; refer to relevant rules, regulations, policies and precedents; talk about alternative solutions; discuss implications of these various alternatives and then suggest a suitable solution and a draft reply. Noting and drafting has, therefore, always been a vital part of decision-making process in the Government.

There is hardly any publication on the subject except for some references in the manuals of office procedures. Hence, this attempt, A book for Government Officials to Master Noting and Drafting.

It is a comprehensive book which talks about various concepts, the significance, features of good and bad notings, and skilful drafts citing examples drawn from actual files. Different exercises, their solutions, and samples of some good file notings and useful drafts make this book valuable for all its readers.